CW01502265

EVANGELICALISM AND THE EMERGING CHURCH

With the Christian church in the west in decline, some churches are undergoing difficult transitions as they seek to become relevant, to both themselves and their surrounding cultures. *Evangelicalism and the Emerging Church* details an ethnographic study of a Vineyard congregation making sense of their Vineyard roots and their growing relationship with the self-proclaimed "emerging church" network. Through a rich account of congregational life and tensions, universal issues are raised such as relating to religious parentage, creating safe places for spirituality, Christian growth and maturity, communication with contemporary culture, and the challenges of identity reconstruction. This book is the first to conduct an academic study of a Vineyard congregation in the United Kingdom.

Explorations in Practical, Pastoral and Empirical Theology

Series Editors: Leslie J. Francis, University of Warwick, UK
and Jeff Astley, Director of the North of England
Institute for Christian Education, UK

Theological reflection on the church's practice is now recognised as a significant element in theological studies in the academy and seminary. Ashgate's new series in practical, pastoral and empirical theology seeks to foster this resurgence of interest and encourage new developments in practical and applied aspects of theology worldwide. This timely series draws together a wide range of disciplinary approaches and empirical studies to embrace contemporary developments including: the expansion of research in empirical theology, psychological theology, ministry studies, public theology, Christian education and faith development; key issues of contemporary society such as health, ethics and the environment; and more traditional areas of concern such as pastoral care and counselling.

Other titles in the series include:

Entering the New Theological Space
Blurred Encounters of Faith, Politics and Community
Edited by John Reader and Christopher R. Baker
978-0-7546-6339-3

Hospital Chaplaincy in the Twenty-first Century
The Crisis of Spiritual Care on the NHS
Christopher Swift
978-0-7546-6416-1

Theology without Words
Theology in the Deaf Community
Wayne Morris
978-0-7546-6227-3

Reconstructing Practical Theology
The Impact of Globalization
John Reader
978-0-7546-6224-2

Evangelicalism and the Emerging Church

A Congregational Study of a Vineyard Church

CORY E. LABANOW

Special Education Teacher, New York

ASHGATE

Published by
Ashgate Publishing Limited
Wey Court East
Union Road
Farnham
Surrey, GU9 7PT
England

Ashgate Publishing Company
Suite 420
101 Cherry Street
Burlington
VT 05401-4405
USA

www.ashgate.com

British Library Cataloguing in Publication Data
Labanow, Cory E.
Evangelicalism and the emerging church : a congregational study of a Vineyard church. – (Explorations in practical, pastoral and empirical theology)
1. Jacobsfield Vineyard (Church : Jacobsfield, London, England) 2. Christian sociology – Association of Vineyard Churches 3. Christian sociology – England – London 4. Jacobsfield (London, England) – Religious life and customs
I. Title
289.9'4'09421

Library of Congress Cataloging-in-Publication Data
Labanow, Cory E.
Evangelicalism and the emerging church : a congregational study of a Vineyard church / Cory E. Labanow.
p. cm. — (Explorations in practical, pastoral, and empirical theology)
Includes bibliographical references (p.).
ISBN 978-0-7546-6450-5 (hardcover : alk. paper) 1. Jacobsfield Vineyard (Church : Jacobsfield, London, England) 2. Jacobsfield (London, England)—Religious life and customs. 3. Christian sociology—Association of Vineyard Churches. 4. Christian sociology—England—London. I. Title.

BX8785.A44L665 2010
289.9—dc22

2008047922

ISBN 978-0-7546-6450-5
EISBN 978-0-7546-9421-2

Printed and bound in Great Britain by
MPG Books Ltd, Bodmin, Cornwall.

Contents

List of Figures and Tables *vii*

1 Approaching the Emerging Church 1

2 Becoming Familiar with Jacobsfield Vineyard 37

3 Hearing the Stories of Jacobsfield Vineyard 59

4 Identifying a Central Theological Question 91

5 Reflections for a Wider Context 101

Appendix A: JV Demographic Survey 129
Appendix B: Semi-structured Interview Questionnaire 131

Works Cited *133*
Index *145*

List of Figures and Tables

Figures

1.1 Tillich's Mutually Critical Correlation 13
1.2 The Practical Theological Cycle 24

Tables

1.1 Growth of Vineyard Churches in the UK 7
1.2 Growth of All Churches in England 7
2.1 JV Demographic Profile 54
2.2 Jacobsfield Demographic Profile vs. JV Demographic Profile 57

Chapter 1
Approaching the Emerging Church

Introduction

"In the UK, [Christianity] is seen as boring," one congregant explained, "but people at JV have realized that it isn't and now want to show others it isn't, so our goal is finding ways to communicate that to people outside church. The evangelism movement emphasized trendy ways of reaching people, but people in our church have realized that those things don't work." She went on to say that: "[w]e're realizing people are into spirituality and we're all asking the same questions about spirituality and the meaning of life, and we want [our church] to say that you might find them where you don't expect them (in church)." Another told me plainly, "Here's my opinion of 'emerging church': Basically, what's happened is that the church has discovered that it's ten years behind everybody else and now it's trying to play catch-up in everything, including life skills."

One declared, "We're challenging the idea that we've got to do something different to reach post-moderns …. Our uniqueness lies in our desire to embody a new story." Yet another remarked, "An emerging church is one that is trying to figure out how to do and be church in a relevant way without having to be held back by the baggage of evangelicalism … but it gets a bit hyped-up to be honest … It's basically just a bunch of guys from different churches writing emails to each other." These are comments taken from interviews of a congregational study I performed of Jacobsfield Vineyard.[1] Despite the variegated opinions arising from members of this congregation about their uniqueness and effectiveness (or the lack thereof), there seemed to be a thread, a common identity, which wove throughout all the sentiments of this self-ascribed "emerging church".

There are numerous statistical records citing the rapid decline of western Christianity.[2] Decreasing attendance, closing churches, and inflexible institutional structures have prompted many to wonder what is next for Christianity in the west. Many reflective practitioners have sought to differentiate themselves from twentieth century Christianity in search of different ways of doing and being church in the pluralistic society of the twenty-first century. Among these practitioners is an informal yet significant network of churches referring to themselves as "the emerging church". Their existence has prompted a number of questions. Why are they discontent? In what ways are they different? In what ways are they the same?

---

[1] Pseudonym.

[2] For such a treatment, see Wuthnow (1997), Davie (1994), Brown (2000), and Woodhead and Heelas (2000).

Will their experimentations ultimately be effective? By what criteria should they be judged? What message do they have for those in mainstream Christian circles? While it would be pretentious to claim that the emerging church holds the answers to the Church's challenges, the investigation of churches intentionally exploring these challenges may help other churches as they search for their own answers. As a result, in this book, I will seek to portray and reflect upon a congregational study of one emerging church, Jacobsfield Vineyard (JV). Examining a single congregation will not yield a comprehensive portrait of the emerging church, but it will enable reflections upon evangelicalism against which the emerging church has reacted and the Vineyard movement with whom JV has a direct yet distanced relationship. Before turning to the methodology guiding the study, it is necessary to first consider the background out of which JV was born.

Evangelicalism and the Emerging Church

Very little scholarly attention has been paid to the emerging church. While not a formal piece of research, Robert Webber's work *The Younger Evangelicals* (2002) does a sufficient job of introducing the outsider to the forces fueling the rise of the emerging church, or, as he terms them, the "younger evangelicals".[3] It effectively catalogues the historical unfolding of this recent movement in evangelicalism composed of these committed yet discontent Christians whom he calls the younger evangelicals. His book gives a brief history of evangelicalism from the Enlightenment, highlighting the emergence of fundamentalism in the early twentieth century and its later strands. However, he focuses much of his attention on evangelicalism since 1950, utilizing three categories which—though overly simplistic—may be helpful for the aims of this book:

- Traditional Evangelicals (1950–1975)
- Pragmatic Evangelicals (1975–2000)
- Younger Evangelicals (2000–?)

He brings the traditional and pragmatic evangelicals under the rubric of "modern evangelicalism" while the third category he sets apart as not only a different era, but also an intrinsically different brand altogether which he simply labels "twenty-first century evangelicalism". He (p. 16) explains that though the twentieth century variety "held fast to a biblically informed and historically tested faith, … they saw it, explained it, and presented it in a cultural situation that no longer exists."

In describing the first group, the traditional evangelicals, Webber depicts them as enculturated in modernity. They maintain the distinctives of twentieth century fundamentalists and see Christianity as a rational worldview grounded

[3] For other accounts of the emerging church, see Riddell (1998), Kirkpatrick, Pierson and Riddell (2000), Tomlinson (1996), Sweet (1999), Rabey (2001), Crouch (2004), Carson (2005), and Driscoll *et al.* (2007).

in propositional truth. However, their approach to church was based on a stable society, and with the radical changes of the sixties and seventies (the advent of post-modernity[4]), the traditional evangelicals generally opted for the security of the familiar and resisted these changes. As a result, the children of traditional evangelicalism (in both a metaphorical and literal sense) grew up in a world in revolution against the past (especially traditions of all kinds) in which, as the adage says, newer is truer and bigger is better. Paradoxically, this was both the height of modernism and the beginning of its demise, and these pragmatic evangelicals began to reform church practices around such elements as seeker-oriented services, contemporary worship music, and big business/mega-church principles spawned from the church growth movement.

However, according to Webber, even pragmatic evangelicals were still wrapped up in the same theology and entrenched in a modern, scientific worldview. A parallel description offered by James Hopewell (1987, p. 25) notes that they "saw God's salvation occurring in individual souls and thus sought reliable formulas for gathering large numbers of persons into congregations. For dependable, sophisticated techniques [they] turned to organization science." For example, one of the pragmatic evangelicals' leading spokesmen, C. Peter Wagner (1976, p. 41), even likened their approach to a scientific discovery:

> Church growth as a *science* helps us *maximize the use of energy* and other resources for God's glory. It enables us to *detect* errors and *correct* them before they do too much damage. It would be a mistake to claim too much, but some enthusiasts felt that with church growth insights we may even *step as far ahead* in God's task of world evangelism as medicine did when aseptic surgery was introduced [my emphasis].

Pragmatic evangelicals, Webber suggests, distinguish themselves from their parents, the traditional evangelicals, by an ahistorical, innovative approach to ministry which often views Christianity as therapy to answer people's needs. They specialize in generation-specific ministries and pride themselves on extreme cultural sensitivity, attempting to offer their seeking generation an accessible, experiential, and personal faith. Unfortunately, Webber contends, much of this era simply turned out to be their parents' progressivist Christianity driven by modern consumerism. When pragmatically-minded evangelicals encounter post-modernism, they have often countered it with sociological adaptation to culture,

---

4 While it is recognized that there is dispute over the legitimacy of the existence of modernity and post-modernity, these constructs are clearly significant to the advocates of the emerging church. Consequently, the concepts of post-modernism will not be imposed on the emerging church, but will be used when recounting their self-ascribed identity. For academic discussions of post-modernism, see Anderson (1992, 1995), Harvey (1989), Gergen (1991), Garvin (1980) and Lyotard (1984). For a critical treatment of post-modernity as merely a new form of western oppression, see Sardar (1997).

viewing post-modernism as a necessary medium to master in order to perpetuate their modern, proposition-based version of Christianity. Yet this group, despite its commitment to a modern [and sometimes hyper-modern] worldview, by its very presence is an indicator that a climate of discontent and experimentation has settled onto the Church landscape.

Webber (2002, p. 16) thus defines a younger evangelical as "anyone, older or younger, who deals thoughtfully with the shift from twentieth- to twenty-first-century culture. He or she is committed to construct a biblically rooted, historically informed, and culturally aware new evangelical witness in the twenty-first century." The difference between Webber's younger evangelicals and traditional evangelicals is readily apparent, but there is also a significant change from the pragmatic evangelicals because this new wave is not only desirous of updated aesthetical changes, but also posing fundamental questions of identity related to what being Christian entails.

Webber presents his own personal findings from a diverse array of experience and interaction with Christians of all backgrounds. He is very descriptive in his approach to the younger evangelicals and seemingly quite sympathetic toward them. He is careful to suggest that they are a new and rapidly changing group, yet identifiable enough to label and describe. Webber organizes his book around 14 various topics (for example, worship, attitude toward history, education, evangelism, and so on) in which younger evangelicals have undergone significant shifts. For example, they hold a postmodern worldview (though he fails to indicate more specifically what he means by this), believe that the road to the future runs through the past, view Christianity as a community of faith (as opposed to a rational worldview or system of therapy), prefer smaller and intercultural churches, lean toward team ministry and decentralized leadership and are very concerned with the plight of the poor.[5]

The weakness of Webber's book is its lack of systematic research. It is more a compilation of observations from a sympathetic observer than the results of an academic analysis. However, the breadth and ambiguity is helpful insofar as it highlights the decentralized and fluid nature of this identifiable, non-institutionalized network of Christians. The force for the younger evangelicals' churches lies mainly in the innovations and vision of local church leaders and then spreads primarily through relational connections and conversational friendships via email, web sites, or interpersonal contact. It has common themes, but no hierarchical leaders. Yet the unfolding landscape of such churches is scantily explored, let alone studied in depth.

---

[5] For an evangelical critique of the emerging church, see Carson (2005). He gives a similar account for the motivations of those within the emerging church, namely the shift in cultural climate and failures of evangelical Christianity. He focuses his criticism primarily upon the emerging church's epistemological affinity with post-modernism and their complete rejection of modernism, arguing that this bias is naïve and unhelpful for Christian truth. See also a similar critique by Colson (2003).

One primary spokesman for the emerging church, though not formally affiliated with the specific network with which JV identify, is Spencer Burke (2003). After spending 18 years in ministry, including a pastoral position in a wealthy mega-church on America's west coast, he came to grips with what he describes as Spiritual McCarthyism and Spiritual Darwinism. He defines Spiritual McCarthyism as the authoritarian rule by a sole church leader, generally the senior pastor, which results in a deadlock on truth and a near-totalitarian church culture. Spiritual Darwinism, Burke notes, is the idea that bigger is always better, creating a food chain which encourages less successful church leaders to adopt the schemes and ride the victories of the biggest and best experts on church growth. Burke's distaste finally led to his departure from evangelicalism by resigning his prestigious position in favor of forming The Ooze web site in 1998. He describes the emerging church in this way:

> At the dawn of a new millennium, something is oozing just beyond the horizon. The ooze is spreading throughout the world as new churches are burgeoning into existence. These communities of believers are welling up from a new movement of God to reach the postmodern world. We believe that ministry will take on a whole new face as the Church wakes up to the fact that postmodernism has seeped into every facet of our society. And that's OK. In reality, ooze is not easily controlled, harnessed, or restrained. Yet, as we begin to embrace the reality of our times, we have the potential to be a church in transition from modernism to postmodernism. We see our role as not trying to define or direct but to be a search party and tour guides for postmoderns by postmoderns, as we take the ride of our lives together on this spiritual journey.

Emergent Village

Proactive church responses of this kind are mainly identifiable in three regions at present: Australia and New Zealand, the United Kingdom, and the United States. Each of these carries a unique makeup with differing degrees of experimentation and progression. As a general rule (exceptions apply), the Church in Australia and New Zealand is the most innovative and contains the widest range. The United States, on the other hand, has the narrowest spectrum of these regions. Finally, Britain falls somewhere in between these extremes. It has a significantly diverse array of church experimentation—much of it related to the experimental influence of Australia and New Zealand—yet is also earmarked by some of the same timidity of U.S. churches.

One conversational network of special interest for this study is Emergent Village. Birthed in the late 1990s as a child of another network of young Christian leaders, Leadership Network, Emergent Village was spearheaded by a Maryland pastor named Brian McLaren (1998, 2001) whose books had become and continue to be influential in the emerging church. I do not suggest here that Emergent Village characterizes everyone who would classify themselves as belonging to the emerging

Jason Clark

church, but since JV's senior pastor was heavily involved in this network as its UK representative, it was of particular significance for this congregational study.

Change and innovation are at the heart of this network ("conversation" is their preferred term). The Emergent Village web site (2005) speaks of response to the political, philosophical, social, economic, and spiritual transitions taking place in what they call the new post-modern, post-colonial world. Consequently, "we must imagine and pursue the development of new ways of being followers of Jesus …", their web site says, "new ways of doing theology and living biblically, new understandings of mission, new ways of expressing compassion and seeking justice, new kinds of faith communities, new approaches to worship and service, new integrations and conversations and convergences and dreams." Emergent Village thus defines itself as:

> a growing generative friendship among missional Christian leaders seeking to love our world in the Spirit of Jesus Christ. Our dream is to join in the activity of God in the world wherever we are able, so that God's dreams for our world come true. In the process, the world can be healed and changed, and so can we. In English, the word "emergent" is normally an adjective meaning coming into view, arising from, occurring unexpectedly, requiring immediate action (hence its relation to "emergency"), characterised by evolutionary emergence, or crossing a boundary (as between water and air). All of these meanings resonate with the spirit and vision of emergent.

It was through investigating Emergent Village that I came into contact with Jacobsfield Vineyard. Since Matt Lawton[6] was the founder and leader of Emergent Village's UK chapter, I hoped a congregational study of the church he pastored, Jacobsfield Vineyard, would be effective not only as a fruitful congregational study in and of itself, but also an arena in which to explore the emerging church ideas via a local setting. Though the church was planted with strong organizational, theological, and stylistic connections to the Association of Vineyard Churches, it has moved to the point wherein not one of the congregational study's 26 semi-structured interview respondents, when asked to classify their church with a group or groups, said that JV was a Vineyard church.

The Vineyard Movement

Though JV have developed a very different identity than most members of the Association of Vineyard Churches, a brief overview of the organization is necessary to understand their roots as a congregation.[7] It is impossible to recount

---

[6] A pseudonym to protect the anonymity of specific Jacobsfield Vineyard participants, the general label "JVer" has been chosen.

[7] For a sympathetic history of the Vineyard movement, see Jackson (1999). See also Percy (1996) for critical perspectives.

the history of the Vineyard movement without beginning with its founder and longtime leader, John Wimber, who, after seasons of pastoring and teaching, planted Calvary Chapel of Yorba (California) in the late 1970s. Due to Wimber's growing emphasis on miraculous gifts of the Spirit and intimate worship, his church left the Calvary Chapel movement in 1982 to join a handful of churches who labeled themselves "Vineyard". As this fledging group of pastors began looking to Wimber for leadership, the Vineyard movement was born, and Vineyard has since expanded to over 900 churches worldwide. It is typical of Webber's pragmatic evangelicals, highlighted by such things as its emphasis on seeker-oriented evangelism, miraculous and intimate experience of the Holy Spirit, and its immersion in the strategies of the church growth movement. According to figures provided by Peter Brierley (2003), the Vineyard movement has grown significantly in the UK[8] since its inception in the late 1980s:

Table 1.1 Growth of Vineyard Churches in the UK

Year	Churches	Attendance
1990	5	2,025
1995	25	4,355
2000	75	8,085
2002	77	9,700

In comparison with other British churches, this trend is an anomaly:

Table 1.2 Growth of All Churches in England

Year	Total Church Attendance (England*)	Per cent of Population
1980	4,738,700	10.1
1985	4,454,700	9.4
1990	4,320,200	9.0
1995	3,864,500	8.0
2000	3,553,700	7.3
2005**	3,317,700	6.7

* Since all but one British Vineyard is in England, the overall church statistics from England (as opposed to Great Britain) are cited.

** Projected figure.

[8] Interestingly, all but one of these Vineyard congregations are based in England (one is in Scotland).

This amounts to an average decrease of 1,100 attendees per week (1.4 million for the 25 year period). In the midst of this degeneration, Vineyard attendance nearly quadrupled from 1990 to 2000 while the number of Vineyard churches increased from five to 75 during that same period. Though recent figures (from 2000 to 2002) show a slight leveling of growth, it is safe to infer, on the basis of these statistics, that the Vineyard tradition is highly effective as an entrepreneurial movement. With church planting as a Vineyard forte, it is not surprising that Lawton (who himself received nearly all of his post-Bible college ministerial training in Vineyard churches) would be both encouraged to start a congregation and equipped with a promising set of resources for doing so.

From this web of backgrounds Jacobsfield Vineyard was formed in 1997. Yet for a congregational study to provide insights of relevance for Christians interested in addressing the problems the western Church faces today, the inquiry must be guided by an appropriate methodology. For this, I turned to the field of practical theology.

The Starting Point: Practical Theology

In order for a congregational study to be truly effective, the methodology needed to be sociologically rigorous while having a decisively theological orientation. While other academic disciplines (both theological and non-theological) were welcomed and integrated into the interpretive process, ultimately I was guided by the fast-expanding field of practical theology.[9] To understand why such a methodology was chosen, it is necessary to first overview the historical development of practical theology, pay special attention to the model of applied theology against which contemporary practical theology is reacting, examine and critique recent approaches and models of practical theology, and identify the common characteristics within the field. From there it will be possible to explicate and justify the model used in this congregational study.

Overview of the Historical Development of Practical Theology

Duncan Forrester (1999, p. 16) observes that practical theology "as a discipline is comparatively young, but the idea that theology as such is practical has been there from the beginnings of Christian theological reflection." Edward Farley (1983, 1988) has identified various meanings of theology as a genre in its evolution which help to trace the relationship (or non-relation) between theory and practice

[9] The term "practical theology" will be favored over the term "pastoral theology". In contemporary scholarship, the terms have much common ground and are sometimes used interchangeably, though they have differing histories. For fuller discussions of the relationship between practical and pastoral theology, see Pattison and Woodward (2000) and Ballard and Pritchard (1996).

throughout the church's history. The first meaning of theology, which began with the New Testament and continued until the early Middle Ages, involved personal inquiry into the mysteries of divine revelation for the sake of enabling the Christian community to live toward truth. He labels this *theology habitus*, theology as knowledge of God pursued through the disciplines of prayer, study, liturgical participation, and a lifestyle of discipleship. A second type, which Farley calls *theology science*, emerged in the second through fourth centuries as an intellectual response to internal heresies and competitive ideologies outside the Christian community; here theology was a discipline of inquiry and study. Examples from this era include Augustine's joining of Christian doctrine with the philosophical perspectives of neo-Platonism or reconciling Aristotelian philosophy with Augustinian theology in Thomas Aquinas' *Summas*. The next wave of change was impacted by the Renaissance and Reformation due to the freeing of humanistic traditions from theological control. Scholarly study, therefore, had new motivation and resources. Since theology now had to struggle to maintain a legitimate presence alongside "scientific" disciplines such as history, philosophy, or philology, it formed alliances with these other fields and thus *theology [the single] science* became *theological sciences*. As a result, there was a subtle shift in emphasis from knowledge of God to knowledge about God. Farley finally describes a fourth meaning, *systematic or dogmatic theology*, the one in which theology disaggregates into various separated and self-sufficient disciplines and consequently becomes increasingly remote from the practices of the Christian faith in the church and in the world.

The emerging field of practical theology, James Fowler (1999, p. 78) notes, "directly challenges this state of affairs, … forcefully reasserting that theology in any 'classical' era, was an eminently *practical theology*." He continues:

> From this standpoint the letters of Paul need to be seen afresh as inventive, inspired practical theology. There we see Paul initiating and responding with his writings to the challenges of the first Christian communities as they tried to give body and flesh to the new reality that had apprehended them in Christ. We need to see Augustine … as a highly gifted ecclesial leader writing to help make sense and shape responses to a time of great threat and transformation in the Roman Empire and in the Church.

Fowler, commenting on Farley's framework, sees a renewed interest in the mode of theology manifested in *theology habitus*; today's practical theology, he continues, says "that we should be more concerned to imitate their faithfulness and creativity, in response to the divine inspiration, than slavishly trying to systematize and apply their practical theological solutions to our challenges in the present."

The Movement away from Applied Theology

In the quickly diversifying university setting of the late eighteenth and early nineteenth century, theology had split into a conglomerate of loosely related specialized disciplines. To survive, the scarcely-used term "practical theology" became an "applied theology", the technical application to practice of the abstract truths gained from other areas of theology such as biblical studies, historical studies, ethics, or systematic theology. This was an explicit one-way street from theory to practice. The purpose of applied theology was the development of and training (of clergy) in techniques to enable better preaching, pastoral care, or teaching. For such reasons, Friedrich Schleiermacher[10] (1811), sought to give life to practical theology by posing it as the "crown of theological study" with his other two branches of theological study—philosophical theology and historical theology. These three identifiable parts of a supposedly inseparable whole are like a flourishing tree: philosophical theology, the roots, leads up into the trunk, historical theology, which is then outworked in the crown, practical theology. The tasks of practical theology are given to it from philosophical and historical theology; it is, essentially, "applied Christianity". Thus when in the future this book refers to "applied theology", it will do so in light of Seward Hiltner's (2000, p. 29) definition; he says that applied theology "implies that principles are acquired through, for example, study of the Bible or of Christian doctrine and that these are applied in a one-way fashion to acts and functions." Practical theology, in Schleiermacher's vision, is not hermeneutical, but is concerned with the rules, procedures, and methods for the minister to translate into action the knowledge gained in the theoretical domains of philosophical and historical truth. However, Schleiermacher's intentions were to exalt and centralize practical action. In fact, in his discussions of philosophical and historical theology, he repeatedly emphasizes that they occur in and are concerned with the present state of Christianity; after all, the roots and the branches are there to serve the crown of the tree. In his reading of the Christian faith, there is a unity of theory and practice which are, as John Burkhart (1983, p. 46) observes, "simply inseparable sides of an integral reality."

While Schleiermacher's intentions were good, his notion of practical theology did not become the crown of the tree as he had envisioned, and his critics have aptly pointed out the reasons for this shortcoming.[11] Two main criticisms by practical theologians have been ascribed to Schleiermacher's scheme. First, it reduced practical theology to a craft of church management, uncritically accepting the structures of church and ministry and exclusively addressing itself to members of the clergy. Second, this problem was exacerbated by the difficulties of a one-way relationship between philosophical and historical theology (theory) and practical theology (practice). "Such a relationship," Alastair Campbell (2000, p. 79) argues,

---

[10] For an overview of Schleiermacher, see Redeker (1973).

[11] For fuller critiques of Schleiermacher, see Woggon (1994), Browning (1991), Farley (1983), and Burkhart (1983).

"is not satisfactory to either side. On the one hand it removes the independent status of practical theology, making it a subsection of dogmatics, whilst on the other hand it opens systematic theologians to charges of irrelevance and inapplicability from practical theologians. The result of this uneasy relationship was the drifting apart of the two disciplines." In other words, Schleiermacher overlooked the manner in which the practices of the church form the questions which Christians bring to the historical sources.

The awareness of this two-way influence has been amplified in recent years as a result of new views regarding the nature of understanding. When theology seriously engages with this, Schleiermacher's one-way street becomes epistemologically inadequate. Don Browning (1991, pp. 5–6) explains:

> The theologian does not stand before God, Scripture, and the historic witness of the church like an empty slate or Lockean tabula rasa ready to be determined, filled up, and then plugged into a concrete practical situation. A more accurate description goes like this. We come to the theological task with questions shaped by the secular and religious practices in which we are implicated—sometimes uncomfortably. These practices are meaningful or theory-laden … All our practices, even our religious practices, have theories behind and within them … We are so embedded in our practices, take them so much for granted, and view them as so natural and self-evident that we never take time to abstract the theory from the practice and look at it as something in itself.

Burkhart (1983, p. 53) summarizes this tension in Schleiermacher's paradigm, noting that:

> he sees practical theology, finally, as consisting in the consequences and applications derived from thought elsewhere. Hence, it tends to technique. It is, to be sure, deliberative, but not really reflective. And its findings, such as they are, are never permitted to force philosophical or historical theology to reconsider. Thus, quite simply, while thought influences action, action does not really influence thought.

How then can theology deal appropriately with the inadequacy of the applied model? While Schleiermacher still does offer much good to practical theology, it has been these concerns which have oriented practical theologians ever since.

Recent Approaches and Models

In order to understand the current state of the discipline of practical theology and the specific approach I have chosen to adopt, it is necessary to look to the development of practical theology in the post-war period. Though the field has not evolved according to well-defined camps, there are a number of influential authors whose work has helped to shape the landscape.

Thurneyson's Deduction from Scripture

Edward Thurneyson (1962) portrays practical theology as a model for preaching, with the purpose of proclaiming the content of the Christian gospel. While Forrester (1999)[12] appreciates the fact that Thurneyson's model allows for the use of secular disciplines while still orienting its purposes to the church, Forrester concludes that his practical theology is dogmatic, too church-centric, and deductive in nature. He suggests that it is heavily influenced by Karl Barth's (1963) understanding of practical theology in which the starting point is the Word of God after which it proceeds in deductive fashion towards proclamation in the context of the church setting. The first problem which critics posed to this essentially applied theology was that it is too narrowly focused on the activity of the church. For example, Karl Rahner (1968) advocated practical theology as being concerned with asking what God is doing both in the church and in the world with a view to how believers and what he calls "anonymous Christians" should respond; moreover, it cannot fulfill this task without the use of the human sciences as well as other theological disciplines. Despite the helpful aspects of Thurneyson's book, practical theologians since Thurneyson have also brought a second major criticism to this model, namely its unidirectional nature, the same criticism ultimately ascribed to Tillich's model.

Tillich's Method of Correlation

Paul Tillich (1967) proposed a model by which theology can be authentically and effectively correlated with other sources of knowledge. In a rapidly secularizing context, his proposal offered a degree of relevance for the Christian tradition to respond to the questions of society. In contrast to Thurneyson, Tillich's model (p. 62) begins with human experience. "In using the method of correlation," he writes, "systematic theology proceeds in the following way: it makes an analysis of the human situation out of which the existential questions arise, and it demonstrates that the symbols used in the Christian message are the answers to these questions." Consequently, he generated an essentially three stage process: (1) human experience is analyzed via rational reflection (2) to identify broader and deeper existential questions which (3) find their answers in Christian Scriptures and tradition. Tillich's method of correlation introduced to the practical theological scene the need for listening to contemporary culture in all its diversity. He (p. 63) goes on to say: "The analysis of the human situation employs materials made available by man's creative self-interpretation in all realms of culture. Philosophy contributes, but so do poetry, drama, the novel, therapeutic psychology, and sociology. The theologian organizes these materials in relation to the answers given by the Christian message."

Hiltner (2000) offers a critique of Tillich in which he (p. 45) notes that "not everything is yet clear about [his] use of the key term 'correlation' to describe his theological method ... But to what extent is correlation a two-way method?" Hiltner

[12] For a parallel argument, see Campbell (2000).

observes that Tillich attempts to solve this problem by indicating that theology deals with matters of ultimate concern and other disciplines with preliminary concerns. However, Hiltner argues, knowledge of the utmost importance to theology may emerge at any time from a discipline which seems far removed from theology. As Hiltner and other subsequent critics have pointed out, Tillich's unidirectional method was limited insofar as it assumed that it was possible to abstract pure theological truth from Christian Scripture and tradition which was therefore immune to challenge from the questions and answers of the previous two stages.

In summary, while the idea of correlating various sources of knowledge in the theological task has been retained, this tension surrounding one-way correlation has been a dominant theme of the discussion ever since.

Tracy's Mutual Critical Correlation

David Tracy (1975, 1981, 1983) was one prominent thinker who attempted to solve this tension which Tillich had created. "Tillich's method," he (1975, p. 46) argues, "does not call for a critical correlation of one's investigations of the 'situation' and the 'message.' Rather, his method affirms the need for a correlation of the 'questions' expressed in the 'situation' with the 'answers' provided by the Christian 'message' … For if the 'situation' is to be taken with full seriousness, then its answers to its own questions must also be investigated critically. Tillich's method cannot really allow this." Instead, Tracy offers a revisionist model in which contemporary Christian theology is understood as philosophical reflection upon the meanings present in common human experience and the meanings found in the Christian tradition. Consequently, the correlation in Tracy's model is an authentically two-way street:

Exploration of Common Human Experience and Language	←→	Historical and Hermeneutical Investigation of Classical Christian Texts

Figure 1.1 Tillich's Mutually Critical Correlation

Thus he builds upon the element of correlation between the insights of the human situation and theological sources, but specifies that the connection is a mutually critical correlation. This is a corrective response in light of the susceptibility of both sources to various interpretations. When he (1975, p. 76) applies his revisionist model to practical theology, the following definition emerges: "Practical theology is the mutually critical correlation of the interpreted theory and *praxis* of the Christian faith with the interpreted theory and *praxis* of the contemporary situation."

Tracy (1981, pp. 46–7) further justifies his model by suggesting that "from the viewpoint of the Christian message itself, the very claim to have an answer applicable to any situation demands logically that a critical comparison of the

Christian 'answer' with all other 'answers' be initiated." Since, for Tracy, the theologian is obligated to explore how and why the existential meanings relevant to Christian self-understanding are present in common experience, assistance from the "secular" sciences is necessary. While Tracy himself suggests phenomenology as a primary (though not sole) method for this task, practical theologians since him have typically made use of one or more of the social sciences (for example, anthropology, psychology, sociology, and so on).

Tracy's model has become very influential as a mode of theological reflection in the field of practical theology,[13] as well as an interpretive starting point for this study of Jacobsfield Vineyard. However, some necessary clarifications and alterations to his method have been offered in recent years which have influenced the practical theological approach used herein. These will be treated later. Before specifying the conceptual location of this thesis within the current field, it is necessary to first outline some common characteristics among present day practical theology, all of which this congregational study will share.

Common Characteristics of Contemporary Practical Theological Approaches

Stephen Pattison and James Woodward (1994, p. 9) suggest a descriptive definition of practical theology: "Pastoral/practical theology is a place where religious belief, tradition and practice meets contemporary experiences, questions and actions and conducts a dialogue that is mutually enriching, intellectually critical, and practically transforming." As one can see, this description reflects Tracy's revisionist model of theology. However, there is much more to the revival in practical theology than simply the writings of David Tracy; he has not been alone in the quest to broaden the horizons of the theological task to include human experience and socio-historical sources of insight. Literature reflective of this new paradigm in practical theology—or, in many cases, the practical nature of all theology—has emerged from almost every continent since the 1970s. In the U.S., two books birthed by symposia at the University of Chicago, *Practical Theology: The Emerging Field in Theology, Church, and World* (1983) and *Formation and Reflection: The Promise of Practical Theology* (1987), represent well the key voices there. In Britain, the first collection of foundational papers was edited by Paul Ballard in *The Foundations of Pastoral Studies and Practical Theology* (1986) and was followed by a second by Duncan Forrester, *Theology and Practice* (1990). Recently, James Woodward and Stephen Pattison, both British scholars, edited *The Blackwell Reader in Pastoral and Practical Theology* (2000) which engaged with authors from both sides of the Atlantic. Australia and New Zealand are also conversation partners. In the non-English-speaking world, parallel and intersecting discussions have taken place concerning these issues in Germany, the Netherlands, France, South Africa, and Korea. To understand the breadth of the

13 For critiques of liberal-revisionist theology, see Chopp (1987), Lamb (1982) and Metz (1980).

practical theological discussion, the collection of essays edited by Johannes van der Ven and Friedrich Schweitzer, *Practical Theology: International Perspectives* (1999), is an excellent starting point. While there are points of contention, there are also some points of commonality which constitute the core of the field, points which the following sections will address.

The Rediscovery of Praxis

Fowler (1999a) claims that practical theological method has as its starting point some context or contexts of praxis. At the most basic level, the term praxis simply means "action".[14] However, it is much more than action; it is meaning-saturated, reflective action as a carrier of belief. It finds its roots in the Greek concept of *phronesis* which is commonly translated as "practical wisdom". *Phronesis* was used to describe the kind of knowing and ability required for the most esteemed vocation in Greece—effective political leadership. For Aristotle (n.d., p. 102), *phronesis* was a synthesis of reason and action: "a state conjoined with reason, true, having human good for its object, and apt to do." Aristotle elucidated this concept at length, speaking of praxis as a pattern in which action and ongoing reflection continually interpenetrate; engagement in praxis, therefore, bred the quality of *phronesis*. While "practice" may connote a simple, non-reflective, and value-free task, one's praxis refers to the ways in which one both acts and reflects on the practice in an ongoing integrated cycle in order to achieve a desired end. As a result, when this study refers to praxis, it will be speaking of the ways in which actions and practices are expressed as containers and out-workings of belief and meaning.

The Greek understanding of praxis has not been the only variation adopted by practical theologians. The Aristotelian tradition of praxis has influenced the field of practical theology via the political philosophies of Europe, but practical theology has also been heavily influenced by the Marxist understanding of praxis through liberation theology.[15] In Marxism,[16] praxis denotes integrated thought and action for revolutionary change. Marx argued that the philosophers have only interpreted the world in different ways, but the point is to change it. Truth is not found in abstraction from action, but in action, namely action in relation to the process of liberation of the oppressed. When appropriated to the discipline of theology, Gustavo Gutierrez (1979), the figurehead of liberation theology, retains

[14] For fuller discussions of praxis, see Lobkowitz (1967), Bernstein (1971), and Habermas (1973). For the relationship of praxis to practical theology, see the discussions in Swinton (2000), Forrester (1999), Fowler (1999), and Tracy (1975).

[15] For a fuller discussion on the influence of liberation theology on practical theology, see Pattison (1994) and Chopp (1987). While sharing in the priority on praxis, a helpful critique of liberation theology can be found in Moltmann (1975). See also the critique of McCann (1981, 1983).

[16] For a discussion of the relationship between Hegel's notion of praxis and that of Marx, see Bernstein (1971).

the correlational model between current situations and Christian texts, but any findings which do not result in action are unacceptable; this model starts from concrete historical praxis and leads to correct action in accordance with the liberating purposes of God.[17] This latter, Marxist-influenced understanding of praxis will inform the present inquiry by reinforcing a transformative element to the practical theological process.

Fowler (1987, p. 16) explains a blend of these two emphases of praxis,[18] noting that praxis in practical theology has both "maintenance" and transformative dimensions:

> On the one hand, it involves the ways in which a community does its business—the patterns of action and transaction that constitute its accustomed ways of doing things. On the other hand, praxis involves strategic initiatives and intentional action aimed at the transformation of the community toward a more effective realization of its purposes and a more faithful alignment with its master story and vision.

Theology is not something merely cognitive, but is lived, performed, and experienced. Since praxis refers to the ways in which beliefs are expressed through action, the praxis of a church is thus the embodiment of its theology. It can, therefore, be read and reflected upon as a theological "text". As a congregational study examines a church's praxis, it is a thoroughly theological inquiry. However, it must not remain in this dimension of practice. Recent practical theology functions in a cycle whereby the congregation's praxis (reminiscent of the Aristotelian notion of praxis) is reflected upon and critiqued in light of the Christian tradition with the intention of enabling better and more faithful praxis (the Marxist, transformative dimension).

There is some debate within the discipline of practical theology regarding its locus. Under question is whether practical theology is done by the church for the purpose of interreligious dialogue or by the church to enable faithfulness to its tradition. Scholars such as Tracy (1981, 1987), Browning (1976, 1983a, 1983b), and McCann (1983) are very concerned with the public dimension of practical theology. For them, practical theology is executed in an effort to generate a credible voice by which the church converses with the world toward the end of shaping a common life. This task is not merely one amongst others in the scheme of theology; it is the goal of theology. Other authors such as Fowler (1983, 1987), Forrester (1999), Pattison (2000), Swinton (2000), Thomas Ogletree (1983), and Farley (1987) choose to anchor practical theology in ecclesial praxis, the approach adopted here. They contend that while practical theologians may also address other audiences and engage in other intellectual enterprises, insofar as

---

[17] See also Boff and Boff (1987) and Friere (1996).

[18] Another helpful critique and summary of the strengths and weaknesses of orthodoxy and orthopraxis (liberation theology's primacy on praxis) can be found in McCann and Strain (1990, pp. 38–64).

they work as practical theologians they do so in relation to and on behalf of a faith community and its praxis. Tracy, McCann, and Browning make their case on the basis of pluralism; to this Fowler responds with two counterarguments. First, due to pluralism people exhibit high levels of spiritual hunger, thus making it essential that Christians find intelligible, imaginative, and accessible ways to communicate their faith tradition. Second, he emphasizes the need for communities of faith to have metaphorical images of the praxis of God. He thus responds to pluralism not by working towards a common theoretical vision of what it means to be human; instead, he describes his characteristics of a "public church" which, while being deeply and particularly Christian, is unafraid of engagement and cooperation with the complexities of pluralistic societies.

As a result, I have adopted the latter approach, utilizing Swinton's (2000, p. 12) definition of ecclesial praxis: "a dynamic human process of critical reflection carried out by the church community." His view underpins the twofold nature of praxis and makes explicit the responsibility of the Christian community: "Critical and constructive reflection on ecclesial praxis is the process of ongoing critical reflection on the acts of the church in the light of the gospel, and in critical dialogue with secular sources of knowledge with a view to the faithful transformation of the praxis of the church-in-the-world." Ecclesial praxis defined as such will thus be explored in and through the context of Jacobsfield Vineyard.

The Relationship of Theory and Practice

With the revitalization of these notions of praxis at the core, practical theology has been forced to reconstruct the relationship of theory to practice. In other words, if practical theology is no longer applied theology, then what is the role of practice and theory? Furthermore, what does this mean for a congregational study?

To remedy this, a new ontology of understanding has been recognized and assimilated into the discussion, one which sees theory and practice as a whole embodied in lived out praxis. Many practical theologians[19] have drawn upon the hermeneutics of Hans-Georg Gadamer (1989) who argues that application to practice is not something which follows understanding (as in the one-way street of applied theology); instead, understanding is a dialogue in which practice and interpretation exist alongside one another from the very beginning. In his seminal work *Truth and Method*, Gadamer seeks to find philosophical ground for the human sciences by dethroning the theory to practice hermeneutical model championed by the natural sciences. He offers sustained critiques of Dilthey and Husserl, both of whom advocated an emptying or bracketing of personal prejudices/commitments in order to correctly grasp the truth of a text, historical epoch, or action. Not only are these pre-understandings acceptable, Gadamer argues, but they are an integral element in the structure of understanding. Gadamer's hermeneutical structure has invigorated practical theology's preference for praxis because he insists that

[19] For examples of some practical theologians who draw most explicitly upon Gadamer's thought, see Gerkin (1984, 1986), Browning (1991), and Tracy (1981).

practical concerns are brought to the interpretive task from the very beginning, and this inevitable reality is not an obstacle to understanding, but a prerequisite to it. He (2003, p. 305) asserts that:

> we must already have a horizon in order to be able to transpose ourselves into a situation. For what do we mean by "transposing ourselves"? Certainly not disregarding ourselves. This is necessary insofar as we must imagine the other situation. But into this other situation we must bring, precisely, ourselves … If we put ourselves in someone else's shoes, for example, then we will understand him—i.e. become aware of the otherness, the indissoluble individuality of the other person—by putting *ourselves* in his position.

What he advocates, therefore, is a both a recognition and a critical knowledge of one's own horizon.[20] In the context of this congregational study, it was not necessary for me to discount my own feelings; the important thing was to be aware of my own bias, so that JV could present itself in all its newness and thus be able to assert its own truth against my own pre-understandings.

If theories are already tied up in practices, where then is the theoretical dimension to practical theology? Practical theology can note the presence of theoretical reflection in two places. First, there must be an analysis of current practices for the theory laden in them. "All our practices," Browning (1991, p. 6) notes, "even our religious practices, have theories behind and within them … We are so embedded in our practices, take them so much for granted, and view them as so natural and self-evident that we never take time to abstract the theory from the practice and look at it as something in itself." Ogletree (1983, p. 85) notes that in practical theology this abstraction is not an end in itself: "[T]he theoretical [side of theology] does not stand in opposition to practical knowledge. It arises as a moment within practical theology itself, a moment in which, relatively speaking, we distance ourselves from the immediacies of experience … It is a movement that permits us to incorporate the various facets of experience more fully into our knowing, doing, and being."

Second, these findings must enter a mutually critical encounter with the theoretical dimensions of Christian texts and traditions, as well as insights from so-called secular sources (the specifics of this correlation will become clearer in upcoming sections). Practical theology, while distinguishable from them, is not autonomous in relation to other theological disciplines such as systematic or historical theology. Practical theology no longer receives specific orders from their findings (as in the applied model), but it still needs these other disciplines to fulfill its task. As practical theology discovers the meanings and challenges of the contemporary situation, it takes these meanings and challenges to the Christian tradition for a mutually critical conversation. This temporary "distancing", as

[20] The term "horizon" is characteristically Gadamerian; he defines a horizon as the range of vision that includes everything that can be seen from a particular vantage point.

Ogletree says, is not an end in itself, but must return to the local context with a view to transformation.

Empirical Orientation and Need of Extra-theological Disciplines

Why then does practical theology rely so heavily on extra-theological disciplines? Gerben Heitink (1999, p. 266) observes that practical theological research is "hermeneutical by nature, but empirical by design. It is hermeneutical by nature, because the research is directed to a process of understanding: the understanding of the significance of the Christian tradition in the contexts of modern society. It requires an empirical design because practical theological research chooses its starting point in the actual situation of church and society." Consequently, practical theology, by its nature and aims, requires the presence of other, extra-theological disciplines. This is best encapsulated in the task of "interpreting situations".

As demonstrated, in post-applied theology approaches to practical theology a central element has been starting with practical contexts, not theory. While the arguments concerning how and to what extent other sciences should be used in theology are varied, there is a general consensus that the involvement of the human and social sciences is permissible, inevitable, and healthily necessary in order to explore the insights emerging from human experience. In approaching the challenge of performing a practical theological inquiry at Jacobsfield Vineyard, it was vital that extra-theological sciences play a major role in the investigation. Since the praxis of both the church and the world is now viewed as a theological text to be read, conceptual tools for exploring practices and their meanings are required, just as other theological disciplines need the borrowed interpretive techniques of philology, history, philosophy, linguistics, or literary criticism to perform their tasks. Johannes van der Ven (1999), one of the most thorough and outspoken advocates for empirical approaches to practical theology,[21] suggests that the concept of *intradisciplinarity*—the borrowing of concepts, methods, and techniques of science by another and the integration of these elements into the other science—is helpful for describing the way in which theology has and should continue to approach other resources. He notes that theology is an excellent example of this; for example, the moral theology of Aquinas, the Tübingen school in the nineteenth century, or Tillich's systematic theology are inconceivable without the use of Aristotelian ethics, philosophical idealism, or depth psychology (respectively).

While there is debate on the role of the findings thereof, a crucial task for practical theology is the interpretation of situations. Since practical theology locates itself within the realm of human experience, the task of the practical theologian is the effective reading of situations with the intent of reflecting on them in the light of Christian tradition. Farley (1987) argues that the recent correctives to the applied model of practical theology necessitate the skills of effectively

[21] For an excellent critical defense of the place of practical theology amongst the theological disciplines see Ogden (1986).

interpreting situations. As shown in previous sections, the historical development of practical theology has placed a renewed emphasis on a critical correlation with the contemporary context, not merely an application to practice of the theoretical insights gained through study into historical texts. Consequently, understanding tangible, contemporary situations in all their complexity and richness is a necessary prerequisite to the practical theological task. Practical theology begins with and arises from situations, looks to appropriate Christian resources in formulating responses demanded by those situations, and then returns to the local situation with a view to faithful and effective praxis. If a mutually critical correlation model of practical theology poses human experience as an equal dialogue partner with Christian tradition, then it should be explored with the same rigor, care, and intentionality brought to the exegesis of theological texts. While the tools may vary, the thoroughness must not. Furthermore, this correlation asserts that neither set of interpretations—the situational or the theological—is invincible or without need of its counterpart, and both are needed to challenge and enhance the findings of the other. This congregational study seeks to exemplify a healthy approach to theologically interpreting the situation of JV.

Therefore, if situations are to be explored, a helpful definition of "situation" is needed. I have chosen to borrow a definition from Farley (1987, p. 12): "the way various items, powers, and events in the environment gather together so as to require responses from participants." He (p. 10) stresses the importance of interpreting situations because human beings tend to exist within them "in an oblivious way. Most of the elements in situations are experienced as background. Situations or their elements get our attention when they become problematic, pose crises, require decisions. Here, situations evoke self-conscious interpretive response." Practical theology exists to both guide the community of faith when it is conscious of some aspects of its situation due to crisis as well as make it aware of those aspects of its situation which it may be unconsciously overlooking. Farley (pp. 12–14) argues for a self-conscious, self-critical, and disciplined interpretation of situations characterized by four features. The first task is identifying the distinctive and constituent features of a situation because "the components (powers, events, causalities) of a situation are not simply there on the surface. Discerning the components of a situation is not simply like taking a photograph. It is an act of serious and even theological self-criticism." Moreover, situations are comprised of different kinds of things with very different genres (for example, different types of individuals, worldviews, language, futures, and so on) and thus require an identification of the complexities found therein. Second, a situation's past must also be explored, and while Farley does not make reference to it, Gadamer's notion of "effective history" will be used later as a means for accessing the pertinent dimensions of the past to assist in the understanding of the present. Third, a local situation must be connected with other, wider situations impinging on it. Finally, for Farley, since situations demand responses, a theological exploration of a situation must look for the ways in which corruption and redemption are being worked out therein.

Emmanuel Lartey (2000), in his summary of contemporary models of practical theology, makes it clear that all post-applied theology approaches emphasize a central place for the interpretation of situations. In offering his own model, he speaks of "situational analysis" which brings selected perspectives from relevant disciplines to bear on the situation with a view to gaining a clearer understanding of what is going on. It affirms that the God of all truth can be encountered in various disciplines while also admitting that humans are limited in their perceptions, though they should nevertheless endeavor to see as clearly as possible. Thus, for him, interpreting situations entails "collective seeing" and "comparing visions". Another important resource is Robert Schreiter (1985). While he appears hesitant to locate himself within the discourse of practical theology, he is very concerned to encourage the development of situationally-sensitive "local theologies". For him, this involves a dialectic between the gospel (defined as the Good News of Jesus Christ and the salvation that God has wrought through him), church (a complex of those cultural patterns in which the gospel has taken on flesh through lived communities), and culture (the concrete context in which this happens). Schreiter's scheme is essentially the mutually critical correlation model with emphasis on local, as opposed to universal, self-understandings, and has been influential in the field of practical theology.

While the details may vary from author to author, these descriptions of the task of interpretation of situations highlight the fact that due to the revitalized importance of human experience in theological inquiry, an analysis of the complex nature of situations is required, one which cooperates with appropriate extra-theological disciplines. This emphasis on the importance of reading situations played a major influence in the ethnographic approach used in studying Jacobsfield Vineyard. It highlighted the fact that situations require more than superficial description, but also careful and disciplined analysis.

Transformational

A final common thread is the transformational nature of practical theology. In its processes and its desired goals, practical theology aims at transformation. However, there is some discussion as to how, if at all, practical theology can be "normative". Perhaps the field's most contentious area of difference, this issue debates whether practical theology labors under the banner of theological ethics or functions as an aesthetic enterprise. One the one hand, some—chiefly Browning (1983, 1987) and Tracy (1975, 1981, 1983)—advocate that practical theology rediscover itself as a dimension of theological or religious ethics, bringing together the social sciences and theological ethics to articulate a normative vision of the human life cycle.[22] Others, however, see practical theology as more of a transformational game, a conversational testing of the leeway between the Christian tradition and the contemporary situation in an effort to offer unsystematic fragments of insight

22 The fullest critique of Browning's theological ethics is offered by Graham (1996, 2000).

enabling local churches to more effectively and faithfully respond to their contexts.[23] While I chose the latter approach for this congregational study, in both cases the desired goal of practical theology is response and transformation. Practical theology begins with and stays close to the experiences and praxis of local contexts, converses with the theories represented by those practices and the Christian tradition, and in the "end" is very purposeful to return to practice. Practical theology finds its ultimate legitimacy in the currency of practical transformation. Though it does not work toward final, universally applicable prescriptions, it does, however, produce unsystematic fragments of insight which enable churches to better understand their praxis, reflect upon it theologically, and actively respond with critical faithfulness in their situation. It seeks to achieve this goal in a number of ways.

First, practical theology offers insights by posing new and challenging questions to communities of faith and other theological disciplines. Since practical theology mediates between the contemporary social context and the Christian tradition, it prevents theology from becoming desensitized to or unaware of the needs of the world. By asking new and challenging questions of the Church's theological sources, it catalyzes the emergence of new understandings and perspectives because not only must churches approach their resources with new questions, but professional theologians in these other disciplines must then provide perspectives in response to the queries. As a result, the questions and unresolved issues which surfaced during the JV congregational study were of great importance, and in Chapter 5, those challenging questions will be highlighted as potential sources of transformation for other settings beyond JV.

Second, practical theology seeks to cultivate what Farley (1983, pp. 22–3) described as *theology habitus*, or theology as knowledge of God pursued through the disciplines of prayer, study, liturgical participation, and a lifestyle of discipleship. The transformational edge of practical theology therefore seeks to train communities of faith as a whole, and their participants individually, in this *theology habitus* so that they can faithfully respond to the needs of their particular situations. Chapter 5 will also look to the ways in which JV's praxis trains (or fails to train) participants in this embodied life of discipleship and what that may teach other churches.

Third, practical theology relates the questions and concerns of the faith community and its context to its primary vocation: participating in the mission of God. There has been ample theological literature[24] in recent years exploring a missional identity of the Church, and practical theology as exercised here[25] has as its goal critical faithfulness to God's mission in the world. Some practical theologians, such as Browning and Fowler, have developed this idea at length,

---

23 For an overview of this perspective, see Pattison with Woodward (1994), Campbell (2000) and Pattison (2000).

24 See, for example, Bosch (1991), Guder (1998), and Banks (1999).

25 See also Forrester (1999), Fowler (1987, 1999), Browning (1991), Swinton (2000), Swinton and Mowat (2006), Ballard and Pritchard (1996) and Ballard (1999).

relating the mission of God to various metaphors to which Christian action must be related. For instance, Fowler (1987), drawing on the metaphorical theology of H. Richard Neibuhr, finds human participation in the mission of God best exemplified through the metaphors of co-creation, co-governance, co-liberation, and redemption. He then goes on to paint his vision, alongside other authors such as Martin Marty (1981) and Parker J. Palmer (1981), for a "public church" which outworks these metaphors in a diverse and pluralistic world. Whatever metaphors or theological concepts of mission one chooses to adopt, there is consensus within the field that practical theology has the purpose of helping churches find ways theologically to correlate their own efforts at faithfulness with the ways in which God is at work in the world. Consequently, practical theological reflection must press beyond merely understanding a congregation and its cultural situation to envisioning ways in which a congregation may better participate in the mission of God. While it is inappropriate to state definitively what JV or another church must do, some attention will be given to ways in which practical theological reflection may guide this process towards more faithful—though not final—praxis.

Adapted Model of Practical Theology

The following section will relate these characteristics of the discipline to the approach adopted by this exercise of practical theology. I will first offer a definition of practical theology, then the conceptual model which underpinned and guided my inquiry into Jacobsfield Vineyard. Next, I will pose the field of congregational studies as a useful vehicle for this kind of practical theological investigation, and then explicate the necessary dimension of ethnography. Finally, some tensions resulting from the relationship of theology and the social sciences will be explored with the result of further clarifying the intent of the research.

Summary and Definition of Practical Theology

This congregational study has adapted a definition of practical theology spawned from the current field of practical theology. First, I maintain that praxis, defined as the ways in which action is expressed as a container and outworking of belief, is of central importance. Drawing on the Aristotelian and Marxist heritages, practical theology concerns itself not only with the observed and experienced praxis of persons and communities, but also carries the intention of enabling and ultimately working towards more effective praxis. Furthermore, this exercise in practical theology will remain anchored in ecclesial praxis, focused on enabling communities of faith to respond in critical faithfulness to the needs of their contexts and the demands of the Christian faith. Second, I also maintain that practical theology, by its nature and aims, requires the presence of other disciplines, both theological and non-theological, primarily employed in the interpretation of situations. The basic

pattern for this task is a mutually critical correlation between human experience and the Christian tradition.

I have therefore adapted the following basic definition of practical theology: the theological reflection arising out of and giving guidance to a community of faith in the praxis of its mission as it engages in a mutually critical conversation with the situation of the world and the resources of Christian tradition. This definition highlights the interrelationships between four crucial elements of the practical theological process:

- Ecclesial praxis
- Situational analysis
- Theological reflection
- Response

A Model for Practical Theological Inquiry

The following cycle illustrates the pattern which such an inquiry takes:

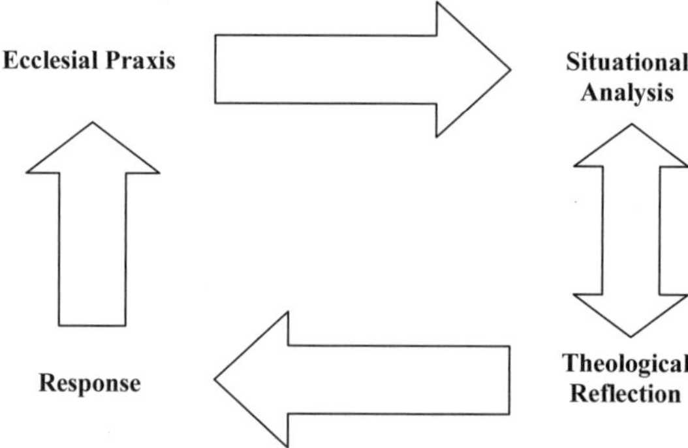

Figure 1.2 The Practical Theological Cycle

Since this model is anchored in the praxis of the church, the congregational study stays close to the experience of Jacobsfield Vineyard. It then carries on a conversation with the complexities of JV's situation, (Chapters 2–4). In Chapter 5, I will give attention to theologically reflecting on these findings. Whether or not one is a member of JV, entering into this conversation should prompt new understandings and points of reflection that can lead to tangible transformation.

However, there are still a number of issues with this model. For instance, the congregational study has not always been a practical theological mode of inquiry, or even a theological one. Furthermore, if extra-theological disciplines are incorporated, importing their own implicit secular assumptions, how will the inquiry retain its theological orientation? Can these disciplines be employed at the researcher's subjective discretion?

Congregational Studies as a Vehicle for Practical Theological Inquiry

While there is a diversity of credible ways in which practical theology can outwork such a model of theologically interpreting particular situations, the following section will suggest that the congregational study is one apt vehicle for doing so, as well as the most appropriate for my research interests. There is an established field of congregational studies, the heart of which is deeply analyzing the situation of one local congregation and the world in which it finds itself. This closely reflects the activity of practical theology. While the term "congregational studies" has sometimes referred to inquiries not associated with practical theology, within the field there are a growing number of practical theologians using the congregational study as a helpful tool.

Before giving further attention to congregational studies, it must be asked why a congregation was chosen as the locus of study, and furthermore why Jacobsfield Vineyard specifically was selected. As Pattison and Woodward (2000, p. 12) observe, generally the starting point for a practical theological inquiry is "some kind of theoretical or practical concern that seems to demand attention." Many times it is a topic of particular interest, such as healing or charismatic spirituality, which catalyzes the study. In this case, I was very intrigued by the emerging church, a decentralized network of frequently-disillusioned yet hopeful Christians claiming to be intentionally rethinking and re-imagining Christianity in a post-modern world. While the stories of individuals are interesting and noteworthy, I was very keen to explore what happens when these Christians collaborate and form churches. With a practical theological model anchored in ecclesial praxis and research interests surrounding congregations identified with the "emerging church", choosing to perform a congregational study of one such church was the obvious decision. This section will review the relevant literature of the field of congregational studies to show how congregational studies have evolved into an appropriate vehicle for practical theology and note how congregational studies benefit the discipline of practical theology.

In their historical account of the field of congregational studies, Allison Stokes and David Roozen (1991) observe that the study of congregations aided by tools of the social sciences has been occurring since at least the beginning of the twentieth century. Many of the early studies were catalyzed by demographic interests, focusing on the church's external social context. The 1960s brought a more prophetic trend to the field, maintaining a focus on social context but with a greater emphasis on renewal and mission. Notable examples in this era include Gibson Winter's *The Suburban Captivity of the Churches* (1961), Peter Berger's *The Noise of Solemn Assemblies* (1961), Conor Ward's *Priests and People* (1961), and Ernest Southcott's *The Parish Comes Alive* (1956). In the 1970s, congregational studies took an inward turn, Stokes and Roozen observe, demonstrating concern with congregational process and what resources for renewal could be found from within the church.[26] Since then, however, questions of how meanings and values form congregational identity and keep it cohesive in the midst of a fragmented world have preoccupied the field.

Despite common interests, the spectrum of congregational studies is still quite diverse. Oddly enough, the discipline of practical theology (or even theology) has not historically owned the method of congregational studies; many disciplines have excavated congregations with their own intentions. A notable example is the volume of essays on one case study, Wiltshire Methodist Church, in *Building Effective Ministry* edited by Carl Dudley (1983). In this influential book, a range of specialists from a diversity of fields studied this upper-middle-class congregation; the research team was composed of four sociologists, two psychologists, one anthropologist, one expert in the history of religion, two theologians, one practical theologian, and three professional church consultants. Their findings sought to demonstrate the richness and multifaceted complexity of congregational culture. *Building Effective Ministry* fulfilled its intention of bolstering interest in congregations as sources of accessible and abundant insight, but this collection of essays lacked a uniform method or disciplinary approach for studying a congregation. Barbara Wheeler (1983, p. 240), a contributor to this volume, notes that "the congregation is an extraordinarily fruitful focus for studies of church life and … it has an identity not fully defined or encompassed by the methods of one study applied to it, whether singly or in combination." On the one hand, this diversity is realistic because a sole method cannot study a congregation in all its complexity. On the other hand, it creates the tension of which method(s) is most suitable to the practical theological task.

Two more recent works have taken a similar approach to the congregational study. Jackson Carroll *et al.* (1987) published *Handbook for Congregational Studies* which was designed as a practical tool for researchers. It offered an interdisciplinary approach with a slightly greater theological perspective. A decade later, a revised form of the handbook, *Studying Congregations: A New Handbook* edited by Nancy Ammerman *et al.* (1998), sought to build upon its predecessor by offering four "frames" or "lenses" through which congregations may be approached and researched: ecology (context), culture, process, and resources. The editors proposed that practitioners who came to the task of congregational studies see the enterprise as an exercise in practical theology. They also added contributions from a wide variety of experts, many of which were social scientists. As a result, the handbook is a reliable resource for research tactics and creative starting points for a congregational study, though not necessarily a comprehensive roadmap for performing practical theology.

Therefore, since Dudley's volume, the discipline of theology (and specifically practical theology) has begun to discover the usefulness of congregational studies. One model of congregational analysis is Hopewell's *Congregations: Stories*

---

[26] See also the helpful historical summary by Woodhead, Guest, and Tusting (2004).

and Structures (1987), possibly the most specific book pertaining to the study of congregations for those with theological and church ministry concerns. He consistently speaks of a local church's "idiom"; more than creeds, governing structures, or programs, it is this which gives a congregation its cohesion. For Hopewell, narrative is the key to understanding the web of signs, metaphors, and rules composing the culture of any group.[27] It is much more than the sequence of events comprising a church's history; it is the story that a group tells to give significance to that particular sequence of events. Churches develop a thick network of construable signs in forming a "local language", or a dialect of signals and symbols.[28] Hopewell offers three features of the relationship between congregational life and narrative: first, the congregation's self-perception is primarily narrative in form. Second, the communication amongst members is primarily by story. Third, by its own congregating, a congregation participates in narrative structures.

Since Hopewell's entire paradigm of congregational study is built around the concept of narrative, he organizes his analysis around the major aspects of narrative: setting (the prevalent world view of the church), characterization (style, behaviors, and values), and plot (the temporal sequence of events the church retells to confirm its identity). Furthermore, he contends that there is also a latent mythic narrative as well; interpretation therefore demands imagination to uncover in what people are saying when they describe their church's story a corresponding myth of the western cultural tradition. This myth can then be used to expose the latent meanings in a congregation, to recount and account for the complexity of a congregation's character. Hopewell asserts that all world views can be categorized according to the four literary genres suggested by Northrop Frye (1957): comic (happy ending), romance (tales of adventure), tragedy (fateful ending), and irony (sober acceptance). From these Hopewell generates four worldviews which congregations use to construct meaning: gnostic (comic), charismatic (romantic), canonic (tragic), and empiric (ironic).

While Hopewell's emphasis on idiom may seem appealing, his critics[29] have argued that it is ultimately his downfall. In spite of the creativity of his application (an uncritical application, his critics note) of narrative structures and Frye's genres to congregations, this analysis does not rise from the empirical setting but is instead imposed upon it. It occupies too prominent a place in his analysis. Congregational life is not identical to "story"; while the storied dimensions of a congregation are essential to understanding it, Hopewell relies completely on literary theory (seen somewhat myopically through Frye's categories) and therefore limits what the congregational setting is able to tell the researcher. Lewis Mudge and James

---

27 For a similar narrative emphasis, see Wind (1993).

28 For an academic discussion, see Douglas (1982).

29 Critiques are given by Dowie (2002) and Browning (1991). Other criticisms not noted here include a lack of attention to his own pre-understandings and the possibility of the myth of a congregation breaking down partially due to the Christian story being told.

Poling (1987, p. 159), while not reacting to Hopewell specifically, summarize this danger well:

> We are called to begin with a "humble"—that is, watchful and listening—hermeneutic which can expectantly approach the signs each community of faith generates in its own setting. For this purpose, it is indispensable that members of the faith community think, speak for themselves, and receive a hearing … Perhaps the best model is that of the anthropologist who seeks to understand a community's culturally coded messages through a process of participant observation *before* imposing analytical categories which originate in the anthropologist's own, academic culture.

While there are other weaknesses in Hopewell's approach, this over-emphasis on narrative precluded me from adopting his method. However, since Hopewell's book has highlighted the legitimately significant role of narrative in congregational life, the JV narratives will be represented and analyzed with great care, but I decided not to impose an outside narrative upon JV.

Hopewell, however, did spark interest in congregational studies as a potential gold mine for practical theologians; furthermore, he stressed the effectiveness of participant observation as an extremely useful research tactic. Practical theologians since then have maintained his emphasis on the congregation and participant observation, but opted for a less prescriptive and less imposing mode of analysis. As a result, an established but nascent vein of congregational studies within the discourse of practical theology is demonstrating the enormous wealth of insight to be gained from an ethnographic approach to congregational studies. It is in this field of inquiry which this study finds itself.

Congregational studies take various formats, though each of these following types has shown how a social science method, oftentimes ethnography, can be utilized effectively in a practical theological inquiry. Some—such as Don Miller's *Reinventing American Protestantism: Christianity in the New Millennium* (1997) or *Building Effective Ministry: Theory and Practice in the Local Church* edited by Carl Dudley—have preferred to utilize the tools of ethnography and other perspectives as means to arrive at broader conclusions. Other authors such as Browning and Hopewell have employed ethnographic practices as aids to articulating a method of theological/congregational research. I will not overextend this research to the assertion of a grand method of congregational study or ultimate conclusions about the wider Church, though some theoretical generalization will follow in Chapter 5. The JV congregational study aspired to be more local in scope and less pretentious in its findings.

Other congregational studies are more idiographic, preferring to examine distinctive congregational acts, or more frequently, single congregations. These works—such as the British case studies found in *Congregational Studies in the UK* (2004), Al Dowie's *Interpreting Culture in a Scottish Congregation* (2002), Mathew Guest's *Negotiating Community: An Ethnographic Study of an*

Evangelical Church (2002), Martin Stringer's *On the Perception of Worship: The Ethnography of Worship in Four Christian Congregations in Manchester* (1999), Stephen Warner's extensive analysis of Mendocino Presbyterian Church in *New Wine in Old Wineskins* (1998), Melvin Williams' *Community in a Black Pentecostal Church* (1974), or Nancy Ammerman's investigation into a fundamentalist congregation in *Bible Believers* (1987)—are excellent examples of local, ethnographic congregational studies, the type and scope this congregational study aspires to be. Why then has the field of ethnographic congregational studies forged a close connection with practical theology? Before giving attention to the dimension of ethnography, I will highlight the benefits of congregational studies for practical theological inquiries.

At the core, congregational studies are valuable to practical theology because they reflect an appreciative approach to the practices and qualities within congregations; they are not to be merely critiqued from the outside but explored and understood from the inside. For this reason, I will adopt Hopewell's (1987, pp. 12–13) definition: "a group that possesses a special name and recognized members who assemble regularly to celebrate a more universally practiced worship but who communicate with each other sufficiently to develop intrinsic patterns of conduct, outlook, and story." This appreciative approach acknowledges and explores the depth and complexity of congregational life; for this reason, writers such as Grierson (1984), Ramsay (1992), Ammerman (1997), Schreiter (1998), Hopewell (1987), or Dowie (2002) in the field of congregational studies often speak of congregations as being and having a "culture", a group's characteristic patterns of action and interaction which hold it together. Recognizing a specific congregation as a subculture acknowledges that it is a unique gathering of people with a cultural identity all its own, though parallels and resemblances with other cultures are expected and inevitable. The above authors highlight the fact that describing a congregation's culture, as a congregational study aims to do, is not a prelude to taking up theological questions, but is integral to that process. Theology, as demonstrated earlier, is not an abstract activity but is embodied in praxis, and therefore is never independent of context. Performing a congregational study is a thoroughly practical theological activity.

To be more specific, Brynolf Lyon (2000) describes four ways in which he sees this recent resurgence in congregational studies as relevant for the work of pastoral theology. First, he notes that congregational studies help practical theology see the dynamics of care within the whole of congregational life, not just the activities of official ministers. This is especially important since practical theology has historically given undue emphasis to ordained clergy as the primary agent of care. In the spirit of Fowler's (1987) term, "the ecology of care", care also exists in the faith community's practices of Bible study, hymn-singing, prayer, outreach, patterns of friendship, the handling of conflicts, the utilization of physical spaces, and the patterns of power and authority. Moreover, the influences are not merely intra-congregational: Lyon suggests that care shapes and is shaped by the market, the state, and civil society at large. Churches are embedded in a wider range of

convictions and practices regarding, for example, family life, gender, and ethnicity. As a result, I chose not only to focus on congregants themselves (with secondary emphasis given to their clergy), but also considered the influences of JV's surrounding context, particularly their position within a post-Christian culture.

Second, Lyon observes, congregational studies may expose the "otherness" within congregational life.[30] Otherness, according to Lyon's usage, refers to the recognition that a congregation is not exhausted by one's sense of what it is or one's wishes for what it might be. It cannot be contained by one's assumptions or the categories of a particular discipline. The JV congregational study, therefore, was open to encountering the unexpected; in fact, I was forced to confront many of my own assumptions and categories as the otherness within Jacobsfield Vineyard was explored. If a congregational study is performed well, it will engender the same experience within its readers.

Third, congregational studies emphasize the nature of theology as something in which the congregation is already engaged, as opposed to the activity of the lone scholar. Communities of faith are theologically active insofar as they make efforts to respond to their situations out of their own interpretations of Christian traditions and their interpretations of the complexities of their circumstances. At JV, the entire congregation was attempting to differentiate themselves and/or their church from evangelicalism, whether congregants consciously labeled this theological activity or not. Though the questions may differ, all congregations are engaged in theology; a congregational study makes this activity more explicit so congregants (and outside readers) can be more critically reflective.

As a result, congregational studies can disclose opportunities for better, more faithful praxis, Lyon's fourth way in which congregational studies are ideal for the practical theological task. Therefore, a practical theological congregational study is undertaken in order to enable effective conversation, in Schreiter's (1998) language, between the implicit and explicit theologies at work in the local congregation. He suggests that explicit theologies are relatively easy to decipher—often they are present in the official doctrines, creeds, or confessions to which a church subscribes. Implicit, or unofficial, theologies are the challenge of a congregational study. He (1998, p. 31) describes them as the "theologies or fragments of theology that inform the congregation's life but are not necessarily acknowledged or overtly expressed." He then describes three reservoirs in which implicit theology can be found: narratives, practices, and texts. Narratives are a congregation's stories which shape and transmit its memories. Practices, such as the utilization of physical spaces, patterns of worship, special occasions, and outreach, also contain implicit theology. Texts, such as vision statements, educational curricula, or promotional materials, though also containers of formal doctrines, can indicate implicit theology as well. The real work of a congregational study is uncovering and exposing the implicit theology of a local church so that it can

---

30 Graham (1996) offers an excellent treatment of the duty of practical theology to attend to otherness and the marginalized.

enter into a critical conversation between the resources of the faith tradition and its praxis. Opportunities for better practice then emerge from this conversation.

Practical theology as exercised through a congregational study can result in the studied congregation undergoing intentional theological engagement. It enables them to name places where their praxis is inadequate and in need of reform. However, since a congregational study is centered on one specific congregation, the difficulty arises as to what, if any, relevance a congregational study has for other churches and practical theologians in other settings. This problem is exacerbated by the introduction of social science methods; practical theology often requires the assistance of social science methods, but the goals of the social sciences and those of practical theology are different. Once ethnography has been discussed more fully, it will be possible to lend careful attention to the tensions in correlating these disciplines.

Ethnography as a Dimension of Congregational Studies

Recent congregational studies, particularly those with a decisively practical theological orientation, usually make extensive use of the method of ethnography. It is crucial, therefore, to offer a basic explanation of ethnography as a social science method; then this description will be related to ethnography's appropriateness for practical theology, further underpinning its pertinence for congregational studies.

Basic Description of Ethnographic Method

Ethnography, like many other qualitative research methods,[31] is well suited to investigate a social group, especially the exploration of the previously unfamiliar. Its forte lies in its ability to produce a rich description and interpretation of the culture of a particular group via an inside-out perspective. The researcher seeks to immerse him/herself in the lives of the participants in their own natural environment in order to define the phenomenon in their terms. Paul Atkinson and Martyn Hammersley (1998), acknowledging the controversies and historical complexities within the field, define ethnography as forms of social research which tend to: (1) place a strong emphasis on exploring social phenomena rather than testing hypotheses about them, (2) work primarily with "unstructured" data, (3) focus on a small number of cases (perhaps just one), and (4) interpret the meanings and functions of human actions (or praxis) via verbal descriptions and explanations with quantification taking a subordinate role. It should also be noted that the term

---

[31] It would be conceivable to study a church issue by way of a quantitative analysis via statistics, but this would provide little insight concerning the meaning of participants' actions. Consequently, this research chose to employ a predominantly qualitative approach. However, a demographic survey was used in order to create some quantitative data which supplemented personal observations and participants' opinions. One recent example of a practical theological inquiry employing a predominantly quantitative approach is Cartledge's (2003) investigation of charismatic gifts. For the strengths of qualitative research, see Denzin and Lincoln (1998) and Bogdan and Taylor (1975).

"ethnography" has a dual usage: it has come to refer to both the method (how the researcher conducts the study) and the product (a cultural description of human social life). As Margaret LeCompte and Judith Preissle (1993, p. 42) say in their work on ethnography, "Ethnographies re-create for the reader the shared beliefs, practices, artifacts, folk knowledge, and behavior of some group."

Ethnography is concerned with the culture of a group. Though "culture" has been defined with great diversity, it usually refers to the beliefs, values, and attitudes that shape the behavior of a particular group of people. For the purposes of this book, I will use the term to refer to that which is cognitively and behaviorally shared by an identifiable group of people having the potential to be passed on to new group members and to exist with some permanency through time and across space.[32] To apprehend this, an ethnographic study involves extensive interaction in the group being studied and results in a thick description of that setting. John Van Maanen (1982, pp. 103–4) summarizes it well:

> The result of ethnographic inquiry is cultural description. It is, however, a description of the sort that can only emerge from a lengthy period of intimate study and residence in a given social setting. It calls for the language spoken in that setting, first-hand participation in some of the activities that take place there, and, most critically, a deep reliance on intensive work with a few informants drawn from the setting.

Consequently, involvement in JV as a participant observer was crucial for me to gather rich, robust ethnographic data. Furthermore, I also employed interviews with 26 JVers to investigate themes in greater depth; the specifics of these data collection techniques will be discussed in Chapter 3.

There is no reason why ethnography as a social science method cannot be applied to a religious congregation. However, it must be asked whether or not a social science method such as ethnography can help a community of faith reach its theological goals. It is vital, therefore, to stress the ways in which ethnography is very appropriate for the discipline of practical theology and the tool of congregational studies.

Appropriateness for Practical Theology and Congregational Studies

First, and perhaps most importantly, ethnography is appropriate for practical theology and congregational studies because of its shared concern for praxis and the interpretation of situations. Eminent ethnographer James Spradley (1980, p. 5) notes that the "essential core of ethnography is [a] concern with the meaning of actions and events to the people we seek to understand. Some of these meanings are directly expressed in language; many are taken for granted and communicated only indirectly in word and action." Clifford Geertz (1973, p. 6), whilst not using the term "praxis", asserts that ethnography is concerned with more than just the

32 Adapted from D'Andrade (1992).

recounting of events. "From one point of view, that of the textbook," he observes, "doing ethnography is establishing rapport, selecting informants, transcribing texts, taking genealogies, mapping fields, keeping a diary, and so on. But it is not these things, techniques and received procedures, that define the enterprise … [It is] an elaborate venture in … 'thick description.'" Drawing on material by Gilbert Ryle (1971), Geertz illustrates this by speaking of three boys rapidly contracting the eyelids of their right eyes. One is doing so involuntarily due to a natural twitch; another is winking to a friend, and the third is mocking the first. From an observation-alone approach, all three movements are identical; however, ethnography seeks to tap into the structures of meaning represented by these actions. As with praxis, action is viewed as a container of theory, or belief.

Perhaps the most sustained treatment of the relevance of ethnography for congregational research and the discipline of practical theology is offered by Dowie (2002). He grounds both practical theology and ethnography in hermeneutics, suggesting that hermeneutics provides a link between the two. Citing the recent hermeneutical developments in practical theology through the influence of Gadamer's ontology of understanding, he follows the influence of this hermeneutical position upon authors such as Farley, Tracy, and Browning. As a result, practical theology is a hermeneutic discipline insofar as it, as demonstrated earlier, is concerned with the interpretation of situations. Ethnography, which he (p. 2) defines as "the social anthropological method of interpreting situations as cultures", can therefore be very useful for the discipline of practical theology. Dowie also grounds ethnography in hermeneutics because ethnographers are directly concerned with the culture of a group; he thus proceeds to adopt a semiotic approach to culture in which culture is viewed as the means by which meaning is constructed and symbols are the carriers or tools which carry and transmit this constructed meaning. Dowie notes that even the ethnographer's role as a participant observer is intrinsically hermeneutical in that the researcher's activity is one of interpretation and that which the ethnographer is studying is the web of constructions which the group uses to maintain meaning and a collective sense of self. Ethnography and practical theology are, therefore, commensurable because they are both hermeneutical tasks.

Ethnography, practical theology, and congregational studies also share a concern for local expression. Ethnography seeks to produce a framework in which to understand and interpret a particular culture within its particular context. When theologically appropriated, ethnography can be a very useful tool; Schreiter (1998, p. 13) notes that such theologically-oriented ethnography's:

> strength lies in beginning with the questions that the people themselves have—not those posed immediately by other Christian churches or those necessary for a systematic understanding of faith. In other words, they try to initiate a dialogue with Christian tradition whereby that tradition can address questions genuinely posed by the local circumstances … leading to a theology enhancing the identity of a local community.

Ethnography has always been concerned with the local and only later, through comparative reflection, with the universal. As demonstrated earlier, practical theology is increasingly framing its findings within such "local" contexts. Practical theology is also concerning itself first with fragments of truth and insight, as opposed to universal norms. It then takes these questions back to its faith tradition so that it can respond most effectively in its local situation. The congregational study seems to be a natural and appropriate union between ethnography and practical theology. However, it cannot be assumed that the analytical patterns and ultimate purpose of qualitative research and practical theology are identical.

The Role of the Social Sciences

While it has been shown that the congregational study blends theological inquiry with social science methods (especially ethnography), the relationship has its tensions. As demonstrated earlier, practical theology has acknowledged its crucial need both for other theological disciplines and the human and social sciences. However, how they are related has not always been clear, and these two fields cannot be uncritically blended together without attention to the ways in which they are incommensurable. James Edwin Loder (1999) notes that the core problematic of practical theology is that it seeks to combine two incongruent, qualitatively distinct realities, the divine and the human, in congruent forms of action. This section will demonstrate that what distinguishes the local findings of the social sciences—specifically ethnography—from those of practical theology is the fact that practical theology has the goal of enabling churches to be faithful to their faith tradition. Ethnography as a method does not have this goal; it is descriptive and interpretive to a certain extent, but has no definite transformational objective.

Proposed Models

Friedrich Schweitzer (1999) outlines three responses or models which have sought to define the relationship between practical theology and the social sciences. The first is the ancillary model in which the social sciences are considered as ancillary, or secondary, sciences. Citing the example of Thurneyson's use of psychology in religious education and pastoral care, this model harshly disregards the secular sciences as relevant to questions of faith, but actively encourages practitioners to draw upon their methods. The positive side of this model is obvious: it preserves the primacy and identity of theology while not excluding valid techniques found elsewhere. However, it narrows the relationship to contemporary culture rather than opening it up, doing little justice to insights from non-theological sources. It has thus been criticized, Schweitzer notes, for its theological absolutism and isolationism.

Second, Schweitzer classifies approaches (such as Sigmund Freud's psychology of religion) which take an opposite stance, that of using social science methods to critique the assumptions and procedures of theology, church, and religion, as a social scientific critique model. Psychological or sociological methods are used to explore the personal and social processes addressed by practical theology. However, there is no room for theology to critique these methods and their corresponding assumptions, thus compromising the identity and unity of practical theology.

Third, there are a variety of approaches which stress intentional cooperation between practical theology and the social sciences, somewhat of a middle ground between the two previous models. Approaches in this category are often called correlational models, and are generally linked with Tillich, Tracy, and other such authors. The relationship is therefore one of mutually critical correlation because both the social sciences and theological sources critique the assumptions of one another. Though I have chosen to use such an approach here, the model of mutual critical correlation still has dangers which need to be identified and addressed.

Dangers of Correlation

One primary hazard is the importation of values from the social sciences which may be antithetical to the theological task, even in a mutually critical correlation. The social sciences have not been born and taken shape in a value-neutral manner.[33] Even though directed to social researchers, Robert Bellah *et al.*'s (1985, p. 301) warning is just as relevant for the practical theologian:

> Social science is not a disembodied cognitive enterprise. It is a tradition, or set of traditions, deeply rooted in the philosophical and humanistic (and, to more than a small extent, the religious) history of the West. Social science makes assumptions about the nature of persons, the nature of society, and the relation between persons and society. It also, whether it admits it or not, makes assumptions about the good person and a good society and considers how far these conceptions are embodied in our actual society. Becoming conscious of the cultural roots of these assumptions would remind the social scientist that these assumptions themselves are contestable ...[34]

To complicate matters, practical theology asks these other sciences to challenge theology by helping it better comprehend and reformulate its own self-understanding. As a result, there is concern for the unity of practical theology. Schweitzer (1999) notes that practical theology is caught between two contradictory demands. On the one hand, it feels compelled (and, in his opinion, rightfully so) to preserve its unity by requiring a clear subordination to the role of psychology or sociology, else the question must be asked whether practical theology is just an adopted name for the social scientific study of religion. On the other hand, if practical theology is to fulfill its self-defined task of mediating between Christian tradition and contemporary culture, then it must retain close contact and cooperation with these sciences.

---

[33] See especially John Milbank (1991).

[34] For a discussion of the theological implications of Bellah *et al.*'s hermeneutic of sociology, see Browning (1991, pp. 85–93).

Browning's Central Theological Question

I do not maintain that there is only one way[35] to preserve the primacy of practical theology in a congregational study, but I decided to draw upon a contribution from Browning's (1991) movement of descriptive theology. The weaknesses of Browning's approach have already been mentioned, and while his quest for prescriptive and universal theological ethics is not to be adopted here, he does articulate some helpful means by which congregations may arrive at the theological issues confronting them. In *A Fundamental Practical Theology*, Browning takes the data from two congregational studies (including the Wiltshire Church inspiring *Building Effective Ministry*) and another performed by himself and demonstrates how it can be used in a theological way.

Browning proposes that congregations reflectively consider and apprehend in all their richness the basic theological questions arising from their practices. These questions must find their culmination in one meticulously-generated and meaning-laden "central theological question". This is then, in his later movements of historical theology and systematic theology, posed to the Christian tradition, and acted upon in his final movement. To illustrate, for the Wiltshire Methodist Church, caught between the proposal to build a religious education building and the pastor's desire to own a home rather than live in the parsonage, their question pertained to balancing the needs of their own leaders and members with the needs of others. A second case study, the Church of the Covenant, felt obligated to get involved in the plight of Salvadoran refugees moving into their town even though it was against the law to do so. For them, Browning felt that their question dealt with balancing the requirements of citizenship with the demands of discipleship. Facing discrimination and the threats of inner-city urban life, the Apostolic Church of God's central question was the ethics of the black family. While these questions may seem suspiciously simple, they are actually concise products of a complex process involving a thorough understanding of a local setting.

This is a crucial link to the practical theological process. Ethnography, like Browning's descriptive theology, aims for a thick description of a particular setting. It challenges the assumptions of theology but does not, however, have the capacity to reflect upon its findings theologically; for this, a congregational study needs an orienting force from practical theology. Working toward a central theological question is one helpful mechanism. I assert that identifying a central theological question is one way in which practical theology can be commensurable with the findings of ethnography and qualitative research while maintaining a decisively practical theological orientation. As a result, Chapter 2 will present a narrative of the JV congregational study, Chapter 3 will present the themes which emerged from the research, Chapter 4 will synthesize these into a central theological question, and Chapter 5 will pose these themes and the central question as comparative concepts which other churches may find useful in considering.

[35] For instance, Loder (1999) and Swinton and Mowat (2006) articulate a compelling metaphor by which to understand the relationship between practical theology and the social sciences, the Chalcedon formulation of the human-while-divine person of Christ.

Chapter 2
Becoming Familiar with Jacobsfield Vineyard

Introduction

Chapters 2, 3, and 4 contain the narrative of the JV congregational study, organized in three phases: familiarization, analysis, and interpretation and the central theological question. This chapter recounts the initial phase of the congregational study, in which I sought to acquaint myself with the general characteristics of the JV situation. The intent of the following chapter, therefore, is to provide a thick description of Jacobsfield Vineyard which offers an accessible account through which the reader can understand my encounter with Jacobsfield Vineyard. It will begin with JV's story prior to my arrival, discuss my entry as a researcher and the methods I chose to utilize, and then articulate the first nine months of the congregational study, the period during which I familiarized myself with the church.

Effective History: The JV Story Prior to My Study

The Jacobsfield Vineyard story begins with 34-year-old[1] Matt Lawton, their founding and current pastor. Raised in a large city in central England in a home environment with alcoholic parents, Lawton was converted to Christianity in a Baptist church at the age of 16. Following secondary school, he studied at a Bible college in England where he met and subsequently married his wife Claire.[2] During this time, he also began to desire to plant and pastor a church when he finished his undergraduate degree. However, after finishing university, while many of his friends with similar ambitions had planted churches, Lawton found himself working as a financial advisor instead. Meanwhile, he joined the Southwest London Vineyard (SWLV) led by John Mumford.

A short word regarding SWLV may be appropriate at this point. The church is the first Vineyard in the UK; Mumford, himself a friend of the late Vineyard founder John Wimber, was an Anglican vicar before visiting California during the Vineyard's early years at which time he decided to start such a place in Britain. Mumford has since been the Director of Vineyard Churches Europe and now, after breaking into smaller regions for manageability, Vineyard Churches UK. The

---

1 At the midway point of the study.

2 A pseudonym.

congregation of about four hundred meets in a rented school hall in Putney, a suburb of London. Interestingly, over two dozen JVers are former members of SWLV. To gain perspective on JV's original parent church, I visited a Sunday service in September 2003 at which time they were sending yet another church plant to a London suburb, apparently their eleventh church plant in the last ten years. From the very moment of entering the hall, I noticed that aesthetically there was little difference between SWLV and JV. Nearly all the printed materials, programmatic structure, and service format were identical to JV merely with different faces and names attached. At first glance, JV seemed to be a carbon copy of SWLV. I spoke with one of the members of this new church plant team who told me quite plainly that "this (SWLV) is the basic model, and all other [British Vineyard] church plants vary from this one."

While working full-time and experiencing success in his secular career, Lawton became a worship leader at SWLV. In 1996, he and Claire began actively searching for a city in which to plant a church. Though living in Jacobsfield at the time, they investigated many possibilities around England, but felt uncertain about all of them. Upon returning home from one such trip, they finally realized that Jacobsfield was the place where they felt at home and were most eager to minister. Jacobsfield is a borough in outer London of nearly 180,000 people. While the official UK 2001 census (2004) shows that 70.5 per cent claim to be Christian (16.7 per cent claim no religion at all, and the rest attest to an array of eastern religions), Peter Brierley's (2003) figures show that only 7.1 per cent (a 1998 figure) attend church services. Furthermore, Jacobsfield's churchgoing population dropped 18 per cent (from 15,300 to 12,600) from 1989 to 1998, attesting to a drastically declining trend in church attendance in JV's immediate area.

In early 1997, Lawton began making contacts and held two informatory meetings at his house to explain his vision for what would become Jacobsfield Vineyard. Twelve people initially committed, and in April 1997 they began meeting weekly in homes as well as monthly at the local Holiday Inn. As attendees increased, they increased their monthly meetings to twice and then three times a month, and finally weekly. When JV attained sufficient numbers to necessitate semi-monthly meetings, they moved the location of the Sunday services to a then-newly constructed local school hall in which they still meet. As they moved from 12 to 50 to 100 in the space of a few years, the demands on Lawton's time also increased. Regarding Lawton's aggressive work ethic during these upstart years, one of the original JVers told me, "Some people say, 'If God's in it, it'll succeed!' but in my opinion, that's mostly rubbish because it takes a lot of plain hard work and that's what has grown the church."

This led to the first and, arguably, the most definitive crisis to strike JV. As Lawton sought to keep up with the demands of his pastoral role and his secular career, he began working 100-hour weeks and drove himself into near-burnout. He reduced his job as a financial advisor to three days per week, but eventually his bosses demanded that he either resume full-time or resign. As a result, Lawton quit in the summer of 1999. The very first day he went full-time at JV he, in the words of his customary narrative of this, "celebrated with a total nervous breakdown". For several weeks he did nothing but sleep 18 hours per day and preach on Sundays, nor could he speak with anyone as he lay in bed suffering from panic attacks which he could not stop: "I found myself continually praying, 'God, you can make this pain go away right now … I'm a pastor! I'm not supposed to have these problems!' And during this time, I never once felt God's presence." One founding JVer recalls that "most Sundays he could barely string a sentence together, but he was very open about his crisis." Lawton took medication, but his nervous and immune systems were, as he says, so debilitated that as soon as he arranged for time to relax, his unconscious mind switched off, forcing him to face the reality of his "inner demons and challenges about who [he is] in life."

Lawton cites two major causes for this breakdown. First, he simply calls himself "an idiot" who ignored the emotional problems from his childhood which resulted in being unhealthily driven, a perfectionist, and a workaholic who got involved in lots of unnecessary tasks. It was during this time that Lawton was forced to confront the dysfunction of his family background, a background which included caring for his alcoholic parents from the age of 12 and a father who left when Matt was 16.

The second cause is also a major aspect of JV's effective history. It was during this time that Lawton's theology began to break down as he realized that his Bible college education had not equipped him to provide answers to people's needs. He thus began to doubt the validity of the answers he had been taught. At Bible college, theology to Lawton was "something to do to get a qualification so I could go and do what I really wanted to do, which was to do church." But, as he says, "I knew that I had been captivated by Jesus and my primary desire was to see other people to come to know him, and yet that desire had been turned into a missiological imperative of … saving souls." He was told at a Vineyard conference that the urgency for this was because:

> in the world around us, people, as fast their little legs can carry them, are running straight to hell. And I remember when I heard that … thinking—the first crack within my theological armor or framework—I don't know if I believe that anymore, … the idea that everybody in the world unless they've prayed this prayer and accepted Jesus are going to hell.

This doubt began "to nag away and eat away" at him. Additionally, certain issues in pastoral ethics such as marrying "non-Christians" with Christians or burying "non-Christians" bothered him considerably. The thought which kept reoccurring to him was "God, this is just not working for me." All of these doubts and questions led him, at the time of his nervous breakdown, to ultimately ask the question, "Oh God, have I put the ladder up the wrong wall?"

Lawton is quick to say, however, that JV were "fantastic … Intuitively, some of my angst had rubbed into the rest of the church in a good way so that we had people come to me and say, 'You said it's always OK to be ill, it's just your turn.

Chill out, don't worry.'" During this time, the core group of fifty, as one founding member remarks, "were not disheartened" but "[Lawton's crisis] strengthened us enormously" and "caused us to respect and love [Lawton] more." However, this also proved to be a very distressing time for JV in which they even considered closing, matters only complicated by the illnesses of several other key members. Another founding JVer attending at the time looks back and views this six-month era as a "period of spiritual attacks by the enemy (Satan)". He went on to say that in the overall history of JV, this crisis served to establish the church, and "though we've always received attacks, they haven't since been mortal wounds to the heart … [That experience] made us strong enough to survive."

The last major tangible crisis in the life of JV came during the summer of 2002 when an influential member and ministry leader left the church. He and his wife had a very high profile in JV, serving as two of 12 elders, and led a large home group, a monthly alternative worship service, and occasional Sunday morning services. When the JV leadership decided to hire two assistant pastors (though since reduced to one and filled by a former assistant pastor), this JV leader assumed he would get one of the jobs. Lawton decided to hand the interview process over to the eldership. After the elders interviewed the candidates, they felt uneasy about hiring him and therefore denied him the position. This JVer subsequently called the church office and had an argument with one of the elders after which time he was removed from the eldership by Lawton. Due to his high profile, the matter became a church-wide concern and Lawton's leadership was called into question as the elders were forced to decide whether or not Lawton had handled things appropriately. One JVer in the home group which this couple led put it succinctly: "It was really difficult because I had two groups of people who I trusted implicitly both saying different things, and one can't be right!" The elders held three separate meetings with him and his wife to discern the situation more clearly. In the end, the couple decided to leave JV. Lawton personally took the ordeal very hard and the couple's home group took a long time to settle as well. One elder told me of the crisis that "it pulled the elders into a cohesive team" and "affirmed [Lawton's] need for elders." In my analysis, this trial served also to test and legitimate Lawton's leadership on a different plane: though Lawton had established himself as a leader vulnerable to their common weaknesses, doubts, and struggles, was his judgment to be trusted in spite of unpopular or unclear decisions affecting highly valued members of the church community?

The Role of the Participant Observer

Entering the JV Setting

Approximately six months prior to the study, I contacted and subsequently met with Lawton in order to explain the intentions of the congregational study and request permission to enter the congregation as both a member and a researcher.

At that point, ethical agreements were made. While Lawton obviously needed to grant permission for the researcher to use the findings in a Ph.D. dissertation and subsequent writings, he was also asked to express any other concerns he might have. This was an important part of the research process which formally established the nature of the relationship between participation and observation. Lawton requested that I become fully involved in the life of the church in terms of service, attending meetings, and developing community-based relationships. He also asked that the identity of congregants remain anonymous and unrecognizable in the final drafts. This meant not only anonymity of names, but also the avoidance of any detailed description of specific church members which could lead to their identification. Finally the pastor requested that the study be, to some degree, a joint venture between the leadership of the church and myself, namely via some mutually beneficial editorial collaboration. These ethical considerations were agreed upon and later drawn into a formal contract which also related to the allocation of pertinent publishing rights.

Though Lawton informed the church's lay leaders of my intentions as a researcher, the Jacobsfield Vineyard congregation was not publicly made aware of my research role until several months into the study. Nevertheless, I was open with JVers in conversations about my role as a researcher, and very clear with all interviewees of my intentions. Though there was some mild hesitation at first, after a few months of becoming assimilated into the weekly patterns of the church, JVers appeared to become desensitized to my presence. I seemed to be perceived foremost as a fellow church participant, though the research project was acknowledged as part of my purpose.

Several months after Lawton's relational estrangement with the leading lay member, I began my fieldwork with Jacobsfield Vineyard, starting in May 2003 and continuing until July 2004. During these 15 months, I infused myself into the life of the community, adopting every role and responsibility expected of its members. Specifically, this entailed weekly attendance at their Sunday gatherings, regular participation in a midweek house group, monthly volunteer work in their community furniture project, taking part in church-sponsored functions, and frequent unofficial social gatherings. Altogether, I became just as (if not more) immersed in the life of JV than the average participant, personally interacting with them individually or collectively about three to four times per week (roughly 15–20 hours per week). The remaining hours of my work week were spent maintaining and classifying fieldwork notes, investigating themes through other sources, and writing up my findings.

The Strengths and Dangers of Fore-understandings

To what an extent should a researcher's own history and perceptions play a role in a congregational study? Fortunately, due to the new epistemological landscape of the latter half of the twentieth century (as explicated by thinkers such as Gadamer), presuppositions are no longer viewed as a hindrance to the researcher. Instead, they are an integral, ongoing element in the interpretive process. When describing a congregation, Browning (1991, p. 62) proposes:

> that fuller description of [the researcher's] experiences and practices (from the personal to the institutional to the relevant religio-cultural) be more systematically included … If practical theology is a historically situated conversation designed to clarify the grounds for our *praxis*, my history, theological commitments, and personal intellectual preoccupations are relevant to what I see and hear in my conversations with these churches.

Consequently, I understood that my personal experience with the JV situation was not only inevitable, but vitally necessary to creating a useful interpretation. I chose to use the ethnographic method of participant observation partly because, as Timothy Jenkins (1999, p. 11) observes, "there is a humanity common both to the inquirer and to the objects of the inquiry, for both are involved in material, local processes of making sense, and this includes making sense of the other. The universal lies in the capacity of both sides to gain in understanding and capability, to be changed through an event or encounter." In the same way, Hammersley and Atkinson (1983) pose that in some sense all social research is a form of participant observation because one cannot study the social world without being a part of it; hence participant observation is less a specific research technique and more a mode of being-in-the-world characteristic of researchers. Hence, throughout the ethnography I did not neglect my own pre-understandings and self-reflections in my analysis. Doubtless another researcher of even slightly dissimilar background and disposition would emerge from the same setting with different interpretations. This congregational study's aim is to present the intersection of my story with JV's story and the questions which they are addressing. In order to make my reader aware of my own pre-understandings, it is necessary to share some basic personal background information and its implications, both positive and negative.

I personally have special interest in the younger evangelical movement. Having been raised in an Assemblies of God church, I then attended a Christian university of the same fellowship. While being immersed in this university and a volunteer position as a youth pastor, I began to question the effectiveness of evangelical Christian churches and began to hope for and imagine something better. In the fall of 2000, I began to consider the possibility of planting and pastoring a church someday. However, I felt uneasy about simply replicating the forms of church to which I was accustomed. Though I was unaware of other church movements at the time, I began a search for alternatives. I finally encountered the emerging church, a network which seemed to be filled with like-minded individuals, unsure of what they wanted but persistently trying to discover something better.

Consequently, the following presuppositions must be understood. First, at the outset of the study I was a relative newcomer to the "younger evangelical" scene. Though I had read much literature about and from their pioneering efforts, my involvement with JV was my first prolonged interactive experience with a church claiming to be a member of this movement. Therefore, my only other experiences by which to evaluate JV have taken place within the mainstream evangelical church, particularly the Assemblies of God fellowship. Second, I had an affinity with many of the leaders involved in these churches in that: (1) I too was "emerging" from unfulfilling and dissatisfying church experiences and (2) I had a like desire to someday help create or participate in a church community which seeks to move beyond the shortcomings of evangelicalism.

While my fore-understandings and personal history are both inevitable and helpful factors, they also carried the potential to blind me to other perspectives.[3] Executing an ethnography always incites certain problems, most spawned from the observer as a research tool. Though the advantages of extensive firsthand involvement far outweigh the drawbacks, certain observational biases and weaknesses are to be anticipated. These mainly result in an unhealthy selectivity in what the researcher does and does not attend to, encode, and remember, potentially leading to errant and/or incomplete interpretations of the cultural meanings being studied. However, the goal is not to eliminate the researcher's subjective perspective, but rather to employ supplementary measures to ensure the reliability of the data being analyzed. Therefore, participant observation alone—though a major source of data—was not considered sufficient to guarantee the most reliable interpretations possible. As a result, additional techniques of data collection were adopted in order to form a triangulation in which all sources were measured against each other to achieve balance, minimize error, and gain fresh insights from one another. Triangulation clarifies meaning and verifies the repeatability of an observation or interpretation, but it is not carried out with the goal of pursuing final, objective truth. Since methods, presuppositions, and continuous change of the researched all impose an unavoidable subjectivity upon the study, the researcher, the researched, and theory itself must seek to arrive at a "negotiated reality".[4] Thus triangulation itself also bears the marks of practical theology, dialoguing with many voices in order to avoid incomplete and unbalanced conclusions.

Methods of Data Collection

As a means of triangulation, three techniques of data collection were employed in the research: participant observation, survey, and interviews. Each will be discussed respectively with emphasis given to participant observation due to its centrality. Participant observation is characterized by an extended period of intense social interaction between a researcher and the members of a social group in the setting of the latter. Typically it is the main tool of the ethnographer; the primary data generated are the researcher's firsthand observations and interpretations of what is going on around him/her. Therefore, I, consistent with the tradition of

---

3 For an introduction to the difficulties and theories of the researcher/researched relationship, see Stringer (2001).

4 For a fuller discussion, see Denzin (1989).

participant observation, first sought to assimilate myself into the natural life of Jacobsfield Vineyard in order to build a fundamental (though detailed) descriptive narrative of the JV community. To compile such an account with accuracy, I kept a running journal of fieldwork notes; to ensure the highest degree of integrity and accuracy, I recorded the information as soon as possible after the event (or preferably during the interaction itself), then later revised it. Its contents served as the well from which my further interpretations were drawn. Therefore, I included every necessary genre of data. First, running descriptions of formal and informal events and conversations with specific, concrete details were recorded. While everything is of significance to the researcher, I was very intentional to explore the JV culture through Ammerman's (1998) recommended dimensions of activities, artifacts, and accounts. Activities, what a congregation does together, can be seen through such things as their rituals, fellowship, worship, and assimilation of newcomers. Artifacts pertain to the ways in which a congregation makes use of space and objects. Accounts refer to the distinctive language of a congregation, the stories which transmit its history, symbols or images which it uses, and the expressed worldview of its members. While every encounter during fieldwork was noteworthy, these dimensions received conscious attention, as the ethnographic account will reflect. Second, interpretive and analytical ideas about the situation even if they did not directly relate to the research questions were written in my fieldwork journal. Third, I also included self-reflections on my own feelings and subjective reactions. Data collection and data analysis informed and guided one another, both an ethnographic practice[5] and a theological one because situational analysis and theological reflection are conversation partners in the cycle of practical theology.

A one-time demographic survey[6] was completed by the congregation. The survey, though a relatively small source of data, questioned members regarding their demography, previous church experiences, and level of involvement at JV. No conclusions were made on the basis of survey data alone; this tactic was solely supplementary to the other forms of data collected.

Another method of triangulation employed to balance my own observations and reflections was that of interview. The first type of interview used was the informal interview, a method nearly indistinguishable from participant observation because it takes place in the context of short, casual conversations. I frequently employed informal interviews as a means to, as Colin Robson (2002, p. 282) says, "seek clarification about the meaning or significance of something that took place." In essence, I sought to link my perspective on particular events or ideas with those of other participants. Such interactions were frequent and quickly noted in detail in my fieldwork notes. They provided a more immediate dialogue for my observations than the latter type of interview used, the semi-structured interview,

[5] This is also known as the process of "analytic induction" (a method in and of itself), but it did not show itself entirely compatible with the purposes of this congregational study.

[6] See Appendix A for a copy of the survey.

albeit much less thorough and systematic. The semi-structured interviews, executed individually or with couples, were based on general themes and issues which arose out of my initial phase of participant observation, providing a useful opportunity for discovering if my ideas about JVers' self-identity and opinions were correct. The interviews and the survey were designed specifically to work in dialogue with the data generated through participant observation. The dialogue was two-way: while I sought to cross-examine my own observations with other participants, I also tested the declared values and professed meanings against their actual practices. A triangulation between these various sources developed which brought balance, credibility, and validity to the range of data collection tactics.

Jacobsfield Vineyard knew me as both a researcher and a participant. Until I executed the demographic survey, my identity as a Ph.D. student studying their community was never publicly communicated. However, I was transparent with all those with whom I interacted that my involvement in JV was research-oriented. While this may have engendered some infrequent uneasiness at first, after two or three months, I felt that JVers were all but desensitized to my research interests and accepted me as a typical member. This phase of fieldwork generated a large stack of notes from nine months of participant observation; in addition to collecting over 26,000 words of written fieldwork notes, I conducted countless informal interviews in casual situations with JV members, sharing some amount of significant interaction with over a hundred participants. Additionally, I conducted 15 pilot/informal interviews (of slightly varying lengths and emphases) during the familiarization phase of my study which greatly informed and fashioned the design of the formalized questionnaire which I then posed to 26 interviewees in the analysis phase of the congregational study, to be recounted in Chapter 3.

What Are They Doing? (Spectrum of Gatherings and Interaction)

To continue the JV narrative, I entered the life of the congregation in May 2004 just as they were settling into a relatively uneventful summer stretch. During my first few months of observation, JVers were planning in anticipation of changes coming in the autumn. Though home groups, Sunday services, and other ministries were active, no major transitions were executed. I found assimilating myself into the relational fabric of JV very easy; within the space of a month, I was on a monthly setup team rota for Sunday services, involved in a weekly home group, and had a handful of dinner invitations.

One of the first things I encountered upon speaking with JVers was the nearly congregational-wide declaration that "there is a lot more to JV than our Sunday services". In fact, I was intrigued to hear this sentiment from participants at every level of involvement, creating curiosity as to why so many people shared this opinion. After further inquiry, I was told that Lawton makes a very intentional point of expressing this sentiment every single Sunday he is present, and I grew to realize that JVers seldom characterized their involvement at JV by Sunday morning attendance but rather by the strength of their relational connectivity with other JVers. One discovery also provoked reflection upon this subject: JV claim to be a church which 220 adults and 90 kids call home, yet Lawton openly explains that 40–50 per cent of this number are not present on any given Sunday, amounting to an average Sunday attendance of approximately 120. Yet they have 150 consistent volunteers on their monthly rotas, suggesting that their congregation widely shares a high commitment to the church's responsibilities yet does not necessarily express this by weekly attendance at Sunday meetings. Lawton describes Sunday services as "the overflow of all the other activities of the church" or "the hub that connects and empowers all other aspects of our life together." The theme of decentralized commitment seemed to run throughout their communal life. Though not necessarily revolutionary, it does signify a move from an event-centered church life to one which stresses community both inside and outside the "official" context of JV.

Despite this decentralized involvement, describing the Sunday service is the most logical place to begin a treatment of their congregational activity. Throughout the following description, it may be apparent that JV services are aesthetically similar—if not indistinguishable—from other evangelical and (particularly) Vineyard churches. Meeting on Sunday mornings in a rented school hall, JV teams of 30–40 people arrive 90 minutes early every week to set up and prepare for the service. In addition to the adult meeting, JV provide groups for kids up to age 12 which meet during the service for Bible study, worship, prayer, and games. Upon arrival, there are a few greeters to welcome attendees and direct newcomers and answer their questions. There is a welcome table with various pamphlets and brochures, but this tangible gesture is insignificant compared to the welcoming nature of people, very conversational in comparison to other British churches I encountered. On my first visit to JV in January 2003, I was especially welcomed by a woman who, as I later discovered, is JV's Newcomers Administrator. She initially greeted me and conversed with me for a couple minutes, then in a [seemingly] reflexive move, escorted and introduced me to a few other males of similar age and temperament. All in all, I left JV that morning having had meaningful interaction with more than a dozen people, yet I did not feel suffocated or pressured. Later I would learn that in a previous church survey, JV leadership discovered that the primary reason most JVers stayed and became regular participants was due to the welcoming spirit they encountered when visiting Sunday services.

Before the service begins, most JVers mingle in the lobby drinking complimentary teas/coffees and eating biscuits. Shortly after 10:30 a.m., Lawton walks to the microphone and invites everyone into the school's multi-purpose room in which they meet. The school (built only five years prior to the study) is generally very clean, professional, and simple; to this basic atmosphere JV add only the essentials—chairs, sound equipment, a computer projector, band instruments, and a music stand for a podium. It definitely carries the characteristic look of a contemporary, pragmatic evangelical meeting room with its lack of religious icons and emphasis on functionality.

Lawton greets the congregation, invites the Holy Spirit's presence with a short prayer, and gives way to a worship team for 20–25 minutes of singing. It does not take long to discover that worship to JVers is more than a formality or a prelude to the sermon. Rather, it is spoken of and treated as a central activity not simply of the Sunday service, but of the Christian life as well. Nearly all of the songs are contemporary worship choruses, many of which are written and promoted by the Vineyard organization. The mood is generally worshipful and reflective, with slight variations depending on which music team is playing (JV have four teams which play once per month). Generally the band are composed of four to seven members playing instruments as basic as guitar, drums, keyboard, and bass to as various as brass and woodwind instruments. There seemed to be a slight disparity, however, between the energy and demonstration of the worship band and the congregation. Whereas the worship leaders tended to remind me of the expressiveness generally characteristic of pentecostals and charismatics, the JV congregation appeared much more subdued, marked by the external inhibitions typical of conservative Baptist or Anglican churches. This lack of congregational expressiveness seemed peculiar in light of the enthusiasm with which JVers would speak of their affection for JV worship.

Following this first session of worship, the worship leader would inevitably allow for a generous pause before praying. After this time of singing (and occasionally in the midst of it) would be a time of observation for the particular emphasis of the Christian calendar. During the summer months, they began making it a weekly habit, proceeding through the catechism of "ordinary time" by reading through the Psalms of Ascent. Typically, a reader would read the psalm out loud, followed by another reader with a 2–4 minute essay of reflection. Finally, one of the readers would lead the congregation in a corporate reading of the psalm. Since this was a fairly new development for JV, I detected that many JVers showed a mild awkward hesitation of unfamiliarity at first. Occasionally, JV also used this time for teaching about various historical figures in Christian history such as St. Barnabas or John Wesley. As it was explained one Sunday: "We're not becoming Catholic by honoring saints but rather recognizing that they too are part of our Christian story and shared many of the problems we face."

After this, Lawton would then lighten the mood by communicating the flow of the day's service and make a few notices, also making mention of the visitor information sheets on each chair. Lawton then opened a microphone to (pre-determined) JVers with notices to share. This often sparked some rather mirthful memories as various JVers would inadvertently manifest their humorous individuality, Lawton many times playfully provoking them as they went along. On one occasion, a woman representing the weekly "Wendy House" group for pre-schoolers and their parents referred to a special kids tune they often sang, and Lawton suggested she sing it for everyone. And much to the pleasure of everyone, the woman proceeded to unashamedly sing a child's jingle about a spider, motions and all. After these notices, Lawton would announce a three-minute break in which he encouraged everyone to talk amongst themselves while small baskets of sweets were passed around.

Following the break, Lawton would then begin his talk, speaking for approximately 35 minutes, sometimes more. His style of delivery was quite conversational, proceeding through a topically-oriented outline. Most talks were components of a larger thematic series, and he usually began by spending a small but sufficient amount of time explaining how the material fit within the whole. As he proceeded, Lawton would stay somewhat close to his notes but occasionally diverted completely for a brief story. Always his tone was casually paced and more akin to a friendly dinner host than a charismatic preacher. I noticed a consistent—and effective—pattern in his talks, a technique of re-education in which he would pose [what he considered] a reductionistic Christian myth, redefine the truth, and then share a personal story to illustrate the redefinition. For example, one Sunday Lawton exclaimed, "We've often heard that if you come to Jesus, you'll get all your questions answered. But Christianity doesn't answer all your questions, it gives us a shitload more! … Christianity isn't about explanation, it's about living by faith."[7] He then followed this with a personal story to illustrate. In this way, Lawton highlighted typically evangelical assumptions, kindly poked fun at them and/or corrected their extremes, and then painted a new definition of these concepts.

JV's closing time of prayer continually appeared to be an extremely valued practice as well. After (or instead of) these songs, Lawton would then lead JV in a time of prayer with and for one another. Whether this was manifested by asking those in need of prayer to come forward, stay at their seats, or gather in groups, he repeatedly emphasized that praying with others was a regular and significant practice at JV. Following the service, more tea, coffee, and biscuits were made available. Setup teams would start packing equipment away, and JVers often spent up to 45 minutes chatting with each other in the school's lobby.

However, as Lawton teaches, members advocate, and I observed, there is much more to JV than Sunday gatherings. For instance, in an exercise at a leadership development course which I observed, JVers named over forty different ministries which connected themselves somehow with JV. While it would be impractical to describe in detail everything which "overflows" out of their Sunday meetings, I will seek to briefly highlight the remaining spectrum.

JV meet in nearly two dozen various "home groups" three times per month. These groups are designed for adults to meet together for fellowship, the sharing of needs, and spiritual growth. JVers are not assigned to home groups, but they tend to cluster into groups of similar age, geography, and (to a lesser degree) marital status. To the members of the one in which I was most frequently involved, the home group itself seemed to be their most consistent and vital link to the life of JV. The groups are fairly autonomous, each deciding for themselves when to meet and what to do. In addition to these home groups, JV have over forty other groups of typically lesser frequency—prayer groups, same-sex mentor groups, a

---

[7] For academic discussions of swearing, see Dutton (2007) and McErny (2006).

pre-schoolers and their moms' group, a teenagers' group, as well as groups/courses for those in divorce recovery, and so on.

In addition, there was widespread support for the church's community ministry, the Jacobsfield Furniture Project (JFP). Beginning in April 2002, the church took over a local charity which otherwise would have closed. This charity collected and then distributed furniture, toys, and household items to local residents in need. Remarkably, in a short span of time, JFP had their own warehouse, delivery truck, and office space—all staffed completely by volunteers Monday through Saturday, 80 in all. JV leadership encouraged all participating members to help with the Furniture Project at least once a month, and the generous response from JVers enabled JFP to move 55 tons of furniture in helping 284 families.[8] Since it is such a central part of JV, they, by the conclusion of the fieldwork period, renamed it "The Vine Project" because of JV's desire to also provide such things as job training and childcare; the project's coordinator repeatedly emphasized that "this is just a natural extension of our desire to care for marginalized people and influence our community in meaningful ways."

As the summer gave way to autumn (2003), JV experienced a significant though relatively smaller season of transition. On a structural level, JV experienced some numerical growth, and in an effort to facilitate this growth, they rearranged their seating configuration on Sunday mornings to accommodate more people. Yet there was also a notable shift in the praxis of JV, a move towards experimentation with techniques acquired from the emerging church movement. In early September, one JV leader remarked to me:

> This is now a key moment in [JV] history because what is happening … is that we are transitioning from just talking about the emergent theological conversation to actually embodying the emergent theological conversation in our everyday faith and life and the forms of our church. And you're going to see a transitioning of forms, an evolving and a deepening.

Though the changes were not revolutionary, nor did they immediately encompass every aspect of JV life, I began to see this unfolding slowly but steadily, particularly in: (1) Lawton's techniques of teaching and (2) more frequent use of practices of classical Christianity by JV members. Regarding teaching techniques, Lawton began to implement a new style of congregational hermeneutics in which a Bible story would be read, after which Lawton would then take reflections on the story or subject matter from the congregation, display these on the projector screen, and then use those reflections as guides and illustrative material for the remainder of his talk. For example, one Sunday Lawton shared the story of the Resurrection from Luke's gospel. After reading the story, he posed the question, "What sorts of sights, sounds, smells, or emotions come to you as you put yourself in this story?" JVers replied with a wide variety of responses from the feeling of shock

8 Inception through August 2003.

to the smell of grass in the morning. Lawton then reread the passage of Scripture, asking everyone to involve these sensory items as they replayed the scene in their imaginations. Second, the observation of the Christian calendar became a part of JV Sunday services with increasing frequency. When I first arrived, it was an occasional occurrence; as the months proceeded, however, this practice became an almost weekly habit. The observation was always organized and led by a man or woman from the congregation; I was even asked to participate on two different occasions, once even given permission to write my own "reflection". Generally, an explanation of the element of the Christian calendar would be given, followed by a Scripture reading, prayer adapted from a historical Christian, and/or a short written essay on the meaning of the observance for our lives. For a Vineyard church born in the anti-traditional wake of the church growth movement, the existence of this practice itself surprised me.

Additionally, JV launched a conversational course called "Journey" to teach basics of the faith to primarily new, but also seasoned, Christians. Its intent was, as Lawton explained, to "learn how to learn how to be a Christian." I found this course to be the most tangible arena of JV's communal dialogue about critical issues, and in some ways, the most explicit demonstration of their theology, though the course only lasted four months. Approximately forty participants would gather one Sunday night per month in, at first a local pub, then later in the newly rented Church Ministry Centre. With chairs arranged in a large oval, Lawton would welcome the group, emphasizing the fundamental rule for the night: "You are not allowed to say something just because you think it's what Christians are supposed to say." Then he would divide everyone into subgroups of eight to ten people, assign a facilitator, and instruct the groups to allow everyone to "share something about Christianity—anything—which doesn't make sense to you, a question you would have no idea how to answer if someone asked you." Each subgroup would then select one participant's question to share with the collective group. Questions were generated such as "Is it only Christians who go to heaven?", "I've been on archeological digs and found evidence which supports evolution—can this be reconciled with the biblical view of creation?", or "Why is one person healed and not another?" The subgroups would trade questions and then discuss these new queries amongst themselves for 20–25 minutes. After a break, each subgroup would present the highlights of their discussion to the collective whole. An open forum of debate would ensue, lightly moderated by Lawton. The goal was not to arrive at answers, but rather to share viewpoints and personal experiences. I felt wary at first, suspecting that "Journey" would turn into either a series of quarrels resulting in no conclusions and aggravated tempers or expressions of ignorance ended only by the leader stepping in to "give the right answer". Neither occurred. After each issue was corporately discussed for 15–20 minutes, Lawton and the assistant pastor, as those with "theological training", would share how Christians throughout history had explored the same issues as well. Lawton would offer some "here's something to think about" ideas, most of which I recognized from the writings of Brian McLaren, but these were not presented as final answers, but as directions for further thought.

The first major church-wide development which I encountered in my study at JV was the October 2003 opening of their Church Ministry Centre, a more permanent facility to house office staff and conduct small-scale occasional meetings (JV arranged for an open space which could accommodate gatherings of up to 80 people) such as Journey, joint home group gatherings, the spiritual gifts course, parties, or newcomer's meals. JVers on the margins, such as those who only attended a home group or Sunday service at the school, were not affected by the Ministry Centre. While the location of new office space and the subsequent refurbishment did not have frequent pragmatic implications for many JVers besides employees, it did strike me as significant in a few dimensions: (1) Lawton gave thorough and frequent attention to its development during Sunday meetings, especially during the process of raising the funds (£40,000 total) and contract negotiations. I was intrigued at this time by the high degree of autonomy and decision-making power the leadership and wider congregation afforded him during these months. While the elders and trustees apparently had agreed on general priorities (for example, easy access for the disabled, cost parameters, meeting space, and so on), Lawton was seemingly given the freedom to execute the rest as he saw fit. For being such a costly and notable endeavor, I never once heard any negative feedback from JVers about the project itself nor Lawton's decisions. (2) The Church Centre also provoked me to wonder if the attainment of a long-term, well-equipped, and custom-fitted facility might, for a young church plant in which change was more a familiar resident than a sporadic visitor, create a sense of being settled, and perhaps lead to complacency.

Also in the autumn was the series on "Messy Spirituality" which extended far beyond the Sunday morning teachings. The series, which lasted for several weeks, was inspired by Mike Yaconelli's book *Messy Spirituality: Christianity for the Rest of Us* (2001) which Lawton recommended all of JV to read over the corresponding weeks of the series. Remarkably, many did, and the book became a frequent topic of discussion in group encounters I witnessed amongst JVers. Essentially, the book stressed the need for grace for others' problems, acceptance of our own mistakes, and spirituality found in life's "ordinariness" and "oddness". However, I found the book's stance to be a reaction against the hypocrisy and legalism often associated with conservative evangelicalism, manifested by a surplus of narrative illustrations about people who had been rejected by supposedly "spiritual" Christians and subsequently "redeemed" by messy spirituality. While I personally found the book extremely unhelpful and even childish, JVers seemed to adore it. Every time the book came up in conversation with JVers, I forced myself to withhold or mitigate my personal views in order to hear their own. Such feedback, however, was vital in helping me to realize a dominant starting point for the JV identity: a rejection of rejection itself, as well as a strong distaste for superficiality. Most often, JVers had endured negative experiences in previous churches, and there was a recurring strong sense of relief over the lack of formulas and rules for fashioning one's spirituality.

There were two notable developments in JV's life in 2004 (during the final seven months of my fieldwork), one very tangible and the other more subtle. In the spring, Lawton and other leadership announced the eventual expansion of a new congregation in a nearby town. Since Sunday services had nearly reached their seating capacity and other potential meeting venues were impractical, they decided that the best way to make space for numerical growth was the birth of a sister church, to be led by Lawton and 30–40 JVers already living in that community. In order to do this, JV decided to hire a "Senior Assistant Pastor" (beginning autumn 2004) to replace the previous assistant pastor who had left in late February; his/her job, Lawton explained, would be to lighten the administrative aspect of Lawton's role so he could funnel more energy into the new church plant, though he would still retain leadership over JV as well. JVers expressed much enthusiasm for this new church planting venture, though the actual execution of it was not planned until 2005, hence its changes were yet to be actively felt.

On a more intangible level, whereas I had expected the value of experimentation to increase and expand during the remainder of my fieldwork, I actually sensed it decrease. Instead of exploring their priority on experimentation, JV retained some things which had been set into motion (such as ancient-future faith elements), but neglected to explain the reason for them or work towards improving them. What I suspected myself and heard articulated by a handful of JVers towards the end of my ethnography was the sentiment that utilizing these practices served only to retain their self-identity as a church seeking to be relevant, irrespective of the effectiveness thereof. Lawton's sermons on the refashioned identity of Christians began to decrease, the Journey course faded out (instead JV held courses on miraculous spiritual gifts and leadership development), and Sunday services—without the vision of a "church for people who wouldn't normally go to church" being promoted regularly—began to revert slowly into that which a thoroughly churched JV knew best: a typically evangelical style. Unfortunately, this trend did not continue long enough for me to make significant judgments regarding its effect on their central question. My hope for them was that with the summer lull behind them and a big transition ahead (the new church plant), JV would regain their sense of exploratory identity. Nevertheless, this season of gradual reversion did seem to indicate one major lesson, namely that without a continual emphasis on cultivating a new identity, people will tend to retreat into that pattern of being which they know best, and in a church of people reared in evangelical churches, that will likely be in the direction of an evangelical brand of faith.

Who Are They? (Demographics)

Before proceeding to the semi-structured interviews, I will give attention to the social makeup of JV. While JVers would not characterize themselves as a Sunday-only church, I discovered that the only setting in which the fullest spectrum of JV participants congregated was during the Sunday morning service. Since this meeting is the orbital center of the JV social universe, it thus made sense to survey this gathering of JVers in order to best gain a birds-eye view of their overall demographic composition. Thus, on 20 June 2004, with full permission of JV leadership, I conducted a large scale survey of that morning's attendees. It may be observed that this survey took place during the latter half of the fieldwork period. This occurred for two primary reasons: (1) the leadership requested that I become a consistently participating member before conducting any large-scale data collection. (2) Due to busy agendas during the spring of 2004, the leadership could not allot sufficient time for the survey until the aforementioned Sunday. Though this survey did not occur chronologically within the space of the familiarization of my research, it is topically more appropriate to include the results in this section.

The methodology for the survey was as follows. Two sheets of paper[9] were distributed to all attendees in the adult service that morning. The first sheet was a formal letter describing my educational intentions, research ethics, and promise of anonymity. It also included contact details for myself in case any participant wished to request the results or speak with me further about the survey or any aspect of my fieldwork. The second sheet was the survey form with four questions requesting information concerning personal statistics, involvement at JV, and previous church experience. After the typical 25 minutes of worship, Lawton invited me to share publicly the nature of my research, as well as thoroughly explain the correct procedures for completing the survey forms. I was available for questions during and after the service, and the forms were collected in a folder at the rear of the hall. Of the estimated 110 attendees, 82 completed the survey, and only one expressed any confusion about properly completing the form. The only group to whom the survey was not made available were the rota workers operating the children's programs in other parts of the building and the technical workers operating the sound and audio-visual equipment in the main hall. This amounted to approximately 16 individuals; however, as the survey will demonstrate, Sunday attendees manifested a high degree of involvement at JV, making these monthly workers a relatively typical group whose feedback would not have drastically altered the results.

Therefore, it is justifiable to suggest that the demographic profile of Jacobsfield Vineyard is as follows:

[9] Both the survey form and explanatory letter are included in Appendix A.

e 2.1 JV Demographic Profile[1]

Personal Information	
Total Respondents	82
Gender	Male: 40% Female: 60%
Mean Age	38[2] (Range: 19–84)
Marital Status	Married (not previously divorced): 50% Never Married: 31% Separated or Divorced: 7% Divorced and Remarried: 7% Cohabiting in a De-facto Relationship: 2% Widowed: 2%
JV Involvement	
Frequency of Sunday Morning Attendance	Weekly: 78% 3 times per month: 10% 2 times per month: 4% 1 time per month: 4% Less than once per month: 0% Hardly ever: 0% Visiting and do not attend regularly: 5%
Involved in Activities besides Sunday Morning Meetings?	Yes: 88% No: 12%
Level of Involvement in Other JV Activities besides Sunday (of those who answered "Yes" to the above question)	2–3 times per week or more: 25% Once per week: 25% 2–3 times per month: 36% Monthly: 11% Answered "Yes" but did not specify frequency: 3%
Mean Duration of Involvement at JV[3]	3.3 years[4]
Previous Church Experience[5]	
Average Length of Total Church Experience	21 years (56% of their lives)
Indicated Some Previous Experience in These Types of Churches	Anglican/Church of England: 46% Evangelical: 27% Baptist: 23% Vineyard: 18% Charismatic: 13% Pentecostal/Assemblies of God: 13% Methodist: 8% Catholic: 4% Liberal: 3% Miscellaneous (Free, Brethren, and so on)[6]: 6% Unsure: 1% No Significant Previous Church Experience: 9%

Type of Church Directly Preceding JV	Anglican/Church of England: 22% Evangelical: 21% Vineyard: 14% Baptist: 8% Pentecostal/Assemblies of God: 8% Charismatic: 6% Catholic: 1% Miscellaneous: 4% Unsure: 1% No Church Directly Preceding JV: 17%
Of Those 83% Who Had a Church Directly Preceding JV, Reason for Transition	Relocation: 25% Personal (that is, needed a change): 15% Spiritual Reasons (that is, urging of God): 14% Social (that is, not fitting in): 11% Kids Needed Better Place: 9% Stylistic Preferences: 5% Leadership Problems: 5% Questions about Faith: 2% Miscellaneous: 6% None listed: 8%

Notes to table

1 Due to rounding percentages to the nearest whole, not all may add up to 100.
2 I measured age by requesting JVers' year of birth. Since my survey occurred in the latter half of my fieldwork, I chose the turn of the year as a midway point from which to measure their ages. Also, one respondent did not indicate an age, thus this respondent's age was not used in calculating the mean.
3 For perspective's sake, the church was seven years, three months old at the time of the survey.
4 This statistic does not include the four respondents who indicated that they were visiting and did not attend JV regularly.
5 For those four respondents who indicated they were visiting, I chose not to include their *previous* church experience since they did not consider JV their home church. Additionally, these respondents either failed to fill in this section or did so incompletely, so any useful data was negated anyway. Consequently, the following percentages are factored from a total of 78, not 82.
6 The category "Miscellaneous" has been used here and in future places to designate that group of responses which appeared only once.

A few initial reflections on this data are as follows. The general demographic was what I expected for the most part, though both JVers (of all age groups) with whom I shared the results and I were rather surprised with the seemingly high mean age of 38. I surmise that the mean age may have been slightly lower had the infrequent JV attendees, who seem to be of a lower age range than those accustomed to weekly attendance, been more greatly represented. The questions pertaining to JV involvement confirmed my suspicion that JVers perceived themselves as highly committed to extra-Sunday activities. The fact that 78 per cent attested to weekly attendance at Sunday services and an additional 10 per cent claimed to come three times monthly struck me as also rather high. Upon further reflection, I surmised that those who attended less frequently were not only more likely to inflate their estimation, but also less likely to be there for the survey in the first place. It would be inexact, therefore, to say that 78 per cent of JVers are weekly attendees, but it is safer to suggest that 78 per cent on any given Sunday are highly committed to the Sunday service. Thus the survey must not be cast as a comprehensive sampling of the entire pool of individuals who connect themselves with Jacobsfield Vineyard, but a representation of the demographic on a typical Sunday morning. While it does fall short somewhat of an ideal set of data, I do not consider this to invalidate the survey's results; it is simply a distinction to keep in mind.

JV manifested a rich and diverse background of church experience. None of the results seemed to stand out over and above the others. The relatively high percentage of experience in Anglican churches did not strike me as very notable in light of England's religious culture; while it topped the list of churches directly preceding JV, its margin of difference was negligible. The one statistic which did seem noteworthy was the figure of 17 per cent representing re-churched or formerly unchurched JVers ("No Church Directly Preceding JV"). Lawton consistently claimed that nearly two-thirds of JV is composed of previously unchurched new Christians, but this statistic indicated a sizable gap between his estimation and the survey results. While new Christians typically may not have developed the habit of weekly attendance and therefore would not have been fully represented in the survey, it is still safe to cast JV as a thoroughly churched community with a great deal of Christian background accompanied by all the fore-understandings, presuppositions, and effective history attached thereof.

Finally, I will place JV within their surrounding context of Jacobsfield. Due to JV's value as a "community church", nearly all of their members live within the same borough, or an adjacent town. Moreover, there is little difference between the demographic make-ups of these surroundings communities to which the remainder of JVers belong, so for simplicity's sake I have chosen to recount the statistics of Jacobsfield. The following table shows statistics of the borough of Jacobsfield according to the UK's 2001 Census (2004) compared with percentages from the JV demographic survey.

Table 2.2 Jacobsfield Demographic Profile vs. JV Demographic Profile[1]

Category	Jacobsfield Statistics	Corresponding JV Demographic
Population	179,768	Approx. 220 adults, 90 children
Gender	Male: 48% Female: 52%	Male: 40% Female: 60%
Marital Status[2]	Married or Remarried: 50% Never Married: 33% Separated or Divorced: 10% Widowed: 8%	Married (not previously divorced): 50% Never Married: 31% Separated or Divorced: 7% Divorced and Remarried: 7% Cohabiting in De-facto Relationship: 2% Widowed: 2%

Notes to table

1 Due to rounding percentages to the nearest whole, not all may add up to 100.

2 Statistics for marital status are difficult to compare on a completely equal plane for two reasons: (1) the census information for Jacobsfield applied to all people aged 16 and over, whereas my survey applied to those aged 19 and over. (2) The categories did not match up exactly. While the census included all married couples—including remarried couples—in one percentage, I chose to create another category for those "Divorced and Remarried". Additionally, the census included statistics for cohabiting couples in a separate section in which it was discovered that 9 per cent of all households were composed of cohabiting couples. Despite these discrepancies, I think it fair to make general judgments of [dis]similarity with these factors in mind.

The census did not indicate a mean age (JV's mean for adults was 38), but it did provide percentages by age group. Incidentally, the 35–9 group was the most common bracket (8.8 per cent), followed by the 30–34 grouping (8.6 per cent). The census also indicated that 89 per cent of Jacobsfield was white with a fairly even distribution of minority ethnicity; JV are also an almost exclusively white community. Though the UK percentage of divorced persons is 27 per cent, the Jacobsfield figure is merely 10 per cent, roughly equal to JV's 7 per cent. Overall, it would be safe to conclude that JV are a fairly accurate demographic mirror of their surrounding community with the possible exception of a slightly higher percentage of female participants.

Chapter 3
Hearing the Stories of Jacobsfield Vineyard

This chapter recounts the second phase of fieldwork, listening to and exploring the stories of Jacobsfield Vineyard. While continuing my role as a participant observer in the church, I also interviewed a cross-section of JVers in a more formal way in order to investigate the observations from the first phase of fieldwork more fully. This chapter summarizes the feedback gained from these interviews and offers some themes which emerged. It attempts to show that while important disparities exist between the manner in which JV's leadership and JV congregants describe the church, common factors can be seen, stemming from the church's desire to differentiate themselves from their evangelical roots. Why, for example, did not one interviewee describe Jacobsfield Vineyard as a Vineyard church? From this uncertain relationship with evangelicalism other important themes took shape. JV were attempting to generate mutual understandings of what it means to have a "safe" church, in terms of accepting others for being undecided about doctrine, showing hospitality to outsiders, and being welcoming to homosexuals. They also expressed great intention and yet great confusion regarding what it meant to mature in their faiths. This was manifested, for instance, by an avid desire to use the Bible for spiritual growth, but nominal clarity for doing so. Despite these uncertainties, both leadership and congregants alike articulated a desire to retain a connection with secular culture. The next chapter, the third phase of the congregational study, moves toward identifying a central theological question for JV by suggesting that the church was endeavoring to reconstruct a new identity but required more explicit criteria for this process.

Analytical Aids

To aid in this analysis, I have chosen to involve two outside voices—Alan Jamieson's research as recounted in *A Churchless Faith* (2002) and Robert Webber's *The Younger Evangelicals* (2002)—as well as an inside voice, JV's senior pastor's identity-claims, in the dialogue I generated with the semi-structured interviews with JV members.

Jamieson's A Churchless Faith: An Overview

In researching the faith journeys of church leavers, Alan Jamieson (2002) concluded that most people who venture beyond the walls of EPC (evangelical-pentecostal-charismatic) churches do so not as a result of a halt in their faith development, but as a necessary outcome of their maturation as a Christian. Jamieson (pp. 50–51) discovered a first group of "Disillusioned Followers", a title indicating "that these 'angry' and 'hurt' leavers have left the church because of specific [complaints] about the direction, leadership, or level of care offered by the church. But … their Christian faith outside the church remains largely the same as the faith they held to during their time in the church." A second group of leavers had moved beyond this into a new season of faith maturation, a group he calls "Reflective Exiles". Here the journeyer is caught between criticism and loyalty, marked dominantly by "their reflective disposition toward the church they had belonged to, the faith they had received and their future faith direction. (p. 65)" Some Disillusioned Followers would develop into this stage while many would not; however, a fair amount of Reflective Exiles, Jamieson said (p. 77), would grow into a third group which he titles "Transitional Explorers" who "displayed an emerging sense of ownership of their faith." This group is "scouting out or opening up a new faith journey. The focus of such leavers is not on what they have left, … but on beginning to find a new way forward. (p. 79)" The fourth and final group of church leavers Jamieson studied he (p. 94) labeled the "Integrated Wayfinders". They "have to all intents and purposes completed the faith reconstruction work" of the Transitional Explorers, and it is here that "the structure of the faith is complete and the person is able to appropriate it as their own faith system. (p. 95)" Jamieson's research seems significant for this congregational study in light of JV's EPC heritage as well as their attempts to differentiate themselves from it.

Webber's The Younger Evangelicals

While Webber's (2002) book has already been introduced, a couple clarifications may be helpful. Though less research-oriented than *A Churchless Faith*, Webber's observations of the field of emerging churches and their adherents proved to be a helpful conversation partner in the analysis of the data. Comparing Webber's reports on other similar (and dissimilar) experimental churches with the attitude and practices of JV greatly aided the research in understanding and evaluation.

Framework of Leadership Identity-claims

The third voice used to contrast with the interviewees was that of Lawton. In order to properly understand who JVers perceive themselves, it is necessary to first differentiate between who their leadership and formal statements say they are and how their members describe themselves. Making such a distinction serves to create space for exploring questions of how these two horizons are different—if at all—and make room for examining possible meaning(s) in the gap/overlap between leadership and participants' identity-claims.

I chose to look to the oral and written statements of their founding and current senior pastor, Matt Lawton, who, for a number of reasons, is the most influential and central authority figure at JV. "Really, Matt and Claire are the church," one

JVer told me. "You can't talk about JV without talking about them." The following claims are drawn from resources in which he intentionally seeks to describe and shape their identity. Only those statements which correlated with other similar accounts were used. This understanding of their identity will be compared with the accounts of JVers (primarily via the semi-structured interviews) and finally triangulated with my own experiences as a reflective practitioner alongside them. Though Lawton offers no formal master framework for understanding JV, I have chosen to categorize his identity-claims under the following headings: (1) Their Existence within a Post-Christian Context, (2) The JV Relationship with the Vineyard Movement, (3) JV-specific Values, and (4) The JV Relationship with the Emerging Church.

A.3.a. Their Existence within a Post-Christian Context

While acutely aware of post-modernism and its implications, Lawton regularly describes their setting (Britain) as being "post-Christian". Within that context, he admits that the Church's shortcoming has been "irrelevance". From this starting point—the loss of Christian influence in society—he describes JV as a place seeking to explore the questions: "What does it mean to be a Christian?" and "What does it mean to be church?". Furthermore, he sees them as missionaries to their own nation and collectively as a "mission post in a post-Christian country"; while consumerist Christianity has made church into a place to be blessed, Lawton teaches that it is about being sent. Yet he is also quick to emphasize that the Church's task is not only to be relevant or interest the disinterested, but to overcome and invert the bad reputation of Christians. Frequently he describes churches as the last places where spiritually curious people will go to explore their spirituality. By describing their context as "post-Christian", Lawton certainly does not intend to indicate "post-spiritual", but rather he believes that "people's frustration with church is often the flip-side of being let down because they have a real yearning for Jesus and for meaning in their life. And they come to the church and they don't find Jesus."

Hence Lawton is very open about the failures of historical Christianity: "Christianity is a used religion, isn't it? And it hasn't been used very well. We've made the good news into a bad argument." He goes on to suggest that "many people are worried that if they become a Christian, they'd become a worse person." Lawton often criticizes Christians' tendency to exclude outsiders. For example, he uses the story of Methodism to illustrate the concept of "Protestant Exclusion". While the Methodist movement flourished as long as friends passed the faith along and took spiritual journeys with other friends, especially those who were the worst members of society, "it all went horribly wrong" when those "at the top of the chain" started to assume "that being a Christian [was] about having your life all together". And they began to live as if it was all about a legalistic brand of "holiness" and "being righteous", teaching that "you can't be a Christian if you smoke, if you swear—if you do anything, you're a terrible person." Therefore, when Christians tried to bring outsiders into the church, Christians drew lines and implicitly demanded that they become like them before joining "their club".

Lawton teaches that Protestantism has historically motivated people to join their ranks by the exclusionary attitude of "'you're going to hell, I'm not', 'you're a sinner, I'm a saint'", or "we're in, you're not". He likens this attitude to that of the Pharisees in the first century, contrasting this disposition with a "Jesus [who] threatens the world with inclusion".

For this reason, Lawton takes a very re-educational stance regarding Christianity because, for him, the results of these failures "are symptoms of a larger problem: we've forgotten who we are." Thus a huge task for JV, in his opinion, is the recovery and rediscovery of the true identity of being Christian. He asks, "What bad habits have we picked up as Christians and how do we undo some of those?". Lawton suggests that Christians may have to "unlearn" these habits before they can "relearn" effective ones because "to discover what it means to [genuinely] be a Christian, we must wrestle with what we've been taught, especially those things which aren't helpful." Yet this relearning task to him is also a communal venture: "We need to learn to teach each other not to be stupid Christians."

To Lawton, the primary implication of their post-Christian context has always been and continues to revolve around the concept of communication: "In trying to grow a church with un-churched people, we found ourselves asking, 'Why are we not communicating with our culture?'". Lawton regularly teaches JVers that because culture has changed, the way in which they communicate with people must likewise change; moreover, the rethinking should center on both: (1) what to communicate and (2) how to communicate it:

> The [western evangelical] church has a communication problem with our culture and society. And as best we [at JV] can, we want to put up our hands and say 'Yep, there's a problem!' and we're going to try things. We're going to make loads of mistakes, but we're going to try and find out how we can be Christians all over again so that the people we know can know about Jesus and follow him.

In JV's early days, Lawton claims their programs were repeatedly unsuccessful, and it was then that they were "forced to explore … the very content of our message … [that is,] what does it mean to be a Christian and how do we communicate that in a language the people of our emerging culture can understand[?] We realized that the historical church has gone through this process constantly, with theological reflection, so we started to engage in that process."

A.3.b. The JV Relationship with the Vineyard Movement

To summarize Lawton's stance on JV's relationship with the Vineyard movement, it might be said that they are nearly indistinguishable in programs, familiar in values, but "emerging" in identity. Programmatically, they are not unlike any other Vineyard or contemporary evangelical church—small groups, worship teams, Bible teaching, Sunday gatherings, and so on. Yet when planting JV, Lawton decided that the church would be infused with both shared Vineyard values and some values particular to JV. He seldom frames JV as being just another local representative of the Vineyard movement, but instead regularly speaks of "enjoying [their] relationship with the Vineyard movement", interesting in light of the fact that not one interviewee characterized Jacobsfield Vineyard as a Vineyard church when asked to put themselves on a church map.

One of the Vineyard values he often repeats is that "it takes lots of different kinds of churches to reach lots of different kinds of people". Lawton emphasizes that he never intended to grow a church which everyone could attend. Another grafted value is worship, a "priority" which Lawton describes as "accessible" and "intimate". Traditionally, the Vineyard movement has been known for its high priority on the worship experience and creative use of contemporary music, an emphasis which can be traced back to Vineyard's founder, John Wimber, himself a musician. Lawton cites their ritual of praying with and for people at the conclusion of Sunday meetings as another Vineyard value, one which is based upon the "belief that God is here and that when we stand with one another and lay hands on one another that his presence is here—and he touches us and gets involved in our lives." Closely related is Lawton's choice for JV to be "naturally supernatural" and to avoid "loads of weird Christian jargon [such as] 'Are you washed in the blood, brother?'". These shared values seem to reflect those Vineyard distinctives which: (1) pertain to the individual's relationship to God and (2) sought to correct the extremes of pentecostalism.

Despite similar programs and some overlapping values, Lawton points out that "[i]f there is a difference, it might be that [this church] sees its identity as a research and development project for the emerging church and culture, and we have spent a great deal of time in theological reflection." In this sense, the programs and values take on a very unique dimension: "In other words," Lawton observes, "if you scratch below the surface [of our] programs, you might find some philosophical and theological assumptions that are different."

A.3.c. JV-specific Values

A central value Lawton repeatedly emphasized and defined is JV's desire to be a "community church" as opposed to a regional church. Many Vineyard churches, he observes, are composed of a geographically diverse range of people commuting every week to attend services at a central location. While not degrading the worth of that approach, Lawton notes that "[r]ight from the beginning, we wanted to be a community church—a place where we could share our lives and grow old together. We believe that church should be a context in which deep relationships can be formed: a place to share our hopes, dreams, and pain together." He summarizes this intra-community flavor by describing JV as a group of people "doing life together". In fact, of their five expectations for members, four of them are directly communal in nature: attending Sunday services, joining a small group, serving with others, and praying with and for one another; membership is characterized as an "active belonging". The fifth expectation is supporting JV financially.

A related community value which continually manifests itself is the stress placed upon transparency and realness. Lawton suggests that churches are not generally places where people go to be "spiritually resourced", "honest and real with one another", or "to share … doubts and questions". He speaks of a "robust appreciation for the intellect" which "embraces doubts" and results in "a balance between folk theology and academic theology". JV strives to be "real and engaging", a place where people can "take off their masks" because, as Lawton observes, "we're all trying to construct reality: 'What is life about?'". As a result, he has sought to create an environment which is "challenging", to never pretend that JV is a perfect place with all the answers dispensing a Jesus who would meet everyone's needs. Lawton thus conceives of Christian spirituality and growth as a community activity because the "journey with Jesus is supposed to be lived out and developed in the context of growing relationships with others." Moreover, one central reason for their unity, he underscores, is that JVers have seen each other at their best and their worst, a characteristic of a healthy church. This concept of community is so central to Lawton's thinking that in his most concise description of JV, he defines them as:

> A living story: A story about a church where people are allowed to belong before they believe, where people are listened to, not preached at. A church where it is safe to share doubts and questions, struggles, heartaches and pain, along with fun and parties, and relationships full of meaning, purpose and connectedness. At the same centre of this is our belief that we need each other to help us in the pursuit of Jesus as our alternative basis for living and being. We are on a journey, people with a shared mission ….

A.3.d. The JV Relationship with the Emerging Church and Culture

Lawton is also the UK coordinator of a conversational network of younger evangelical practitioners called Emergent Village, so it is not surprising that in addition to their relationship with the Vineyard movement, Lawton claims that JVers see themselves as "a research and development project for the emerging church and culture". Lawton does not claim to be a "post-modern Christian or … trying to grow [a] post-modern church". If Lawton is trying to differentiate himself, it might be in response to disaffected Christians who, in his mind, are being immaturely reactionary in their response to evangelicalism. Essentially, he feels that many contemporary church reformations done in the name of relevance are ultimately counterproductive, just "pissed-off Christians having church for other pissed-off Christians". He also contends that "for many Christians engaging post-modernity, they are doing so sociologically, not theologically or philosophically. In short, is preaching and congregating axiomatic to postmodern church? I think not." He asks, "Why are so many burned out Christians moving away from congregations and have no new Christians in their groups? I think they are responding sociologically."

Lawton never claims to have answers to the cultural challenges posed to the church, but he does assert that JVers are in a state of intentional engagement with culture in an effort to reconnect Christians with culture in meaningful and appropriate ways. In relation to post-modernity, he succinctly states that "'culture' is just a given, it exists, and all we are trying to do is engage with that culture in a way that enables people to become passionate followers of Jesus Christ." He further observes, "One of the freedoms of post-modern theological enquiry has been the realization that we have, by and large, culturally circumcised unchurched people before they can be involved in our church communities." He cites JV's greatest challenge as taking all the emerging church's lessons and applying those to their practices for discipling new Christians: "How do we stop new kind[s] of Christians picking up cultural habits of a previous kind that will alienate them from the very culture they have emerged from[?] How will those followers of Jesus learn the beliefs and practices that will enable them to become lifelong learners of Christ who naturally invite their friends on their journey[?]". Lawton frequently uses some terms to describe this paradoxical relationship with secular culture. One is "resident aliens", a label with which he stresses the necessary marginalization of the church from mainstream culture. He claims that throughout history, the church has functioned best when at the edges of society because there it is harder to be a Christian; furthermore, a primary reason why Christians are leaving churches today is because being a Christian is simply too easy. Additionally, he also stresses the characteristic of being a "counter-cultural church", one which does not seek to out-argue outsiders, but one which seeks to "outlive them" via "a passionate pursuit of Jesus".

He identifies JV more in terms of their relationship with the past and the future versus the present cultural transition of post-modernity, citing Robert Webber's (1999) term "ancient-future faith". Lawton claims that their emphasis on the past may very well be that which makes them a post-modern church:

> One of the problems the modern church brought upon itself was the jettisoning of most of our Christian heritage and culture … We have been discovering that real Christianity has been practiced in all culture at all times, and there is much we can re-appropriate and use to reach our current culture. We see ourselves not so much as new, but as a re-rooting in the ancient, finding our identity in the tradition and authority of the 2,000 year old historical church and Bride of Jesus Christ.

In similar fashion, Lawton also claims that JVers take their cues from a future rooted in God's plan for creation. He speaks of a process of "re-creation" in which "an alternative reality, God's reality, … [is] being formed and forged in our midst". In response, JVers seek to "walk forward hoping that we will experience more and more of that reality in our lives."

The Semi-structured Interviews

As stated, my role as participant observer brought me into contact with well over a hundred JVers during my fieldwork experience, generating conversations with a wide base of members. These semi-structured interviews were a means of more thoroughly and systematically exploring members' identity-claims with a representative sample of the congregation. From the mass of data accumulated in the familiarization phase, I generated a semi-structured interview questionnaire[1] focusing on JVers' personal stories, reflections on pertinent aspects of church practice, and opinions on deeper interpretation-oriented issues. After conducting a handful of "mock'" interviews with JVers to ensure the understandability of the questions themselves, I settled on a two-part questionnaire dealing with: (1) "Basic Reflections on Jacobsfield Vineyard" and (2) "Analysis of Deeper Issues". Therefore, in the latter phase of fieldwork, I used this fuller and more systematic questionnaire (as compared with the looser set of concerns I posed to my interviewees in the initial phase) to perform 26 more semi-structured interviews, the results of which follow. In all interviews from both phases, I deliberately involved a wide cross-section of JVers, seeking input from JVers of all ages, backgrounds, and levels of involvement (including two ex-JVers who were willing to share their stories with me). There was no systematic method for choosing the interviewees; several were members with whom I shared a close relationship and many were not. My central concern was selecting those whom would contribute to a diverse whole. Many of the interviews—which lasted anywhere from 45 minutes to two hours—took place in the homes of the interviewees. Most were performed one on one with the exception of married or dating couples who responded to the questions together; I did, however, distinguish their responses in my notes for further analytical purposes. In the following section, I have constructed a narrative of the interview questions with the reason for their respective use.

Interview Protocol

After recording personal information regarding the respondents' age, gender, marital status, duration and frequency of involvement, and previous church experience, I asked each interviewee to recount to me in their own words the story of how they came to attend Jacobsfield Vineyard. I then followed this query with a closely-related one about what personal needs the JVer felt were being met by the church. Whereas the story of the interviewees' arrival to JV gave me an idea of how they came, I felt the obligation to ask why they remained as members. I sought here to understand what they appreciated about JV and those dimensions which, if removed or negatively altered, would cause them to leave. Following this discussion of their needs, I then returned to a narrative question, inquiring into any crises of faith which the JVer may have experienced and JV's involvement (or lack

[1] See Appendix B for the full text of the precautionary material and questionnaire.

of involvement) in that crisis. I anticipated that tapping into crises would enable me to explore common denominators in JVers' personal histories. I then asked the respondents to comment on the role and significance of four elements of their church-wide practice which appeared to have a significant amount of importance: the use of elements of historical Christianity (for example, Christian calendar observances, prayers, creeds, and so on), worship, the use of the Bible, and the role of doubts and questions. Through participant observation and pilot interviews, I had discovered each of these elements to play a notable role in the life of JV and (most importantly) to hold representative significance.

In the latter half of the interview, "Analysis of Deeper Issues", I sought to prompt JVers for their interpretations on some themes beyond the context of their church. First, I asked them to articulate their view of "spiritual maturity" and relate it to Lawton's teaching series on "messy spirituality" in the autumn of 2003. Following that, I attempted to investigate the church's self-articulated relationship with other wings of the Christian Church. In my pilot interviews, I had specifically asked about JV's relationship with evangelicalism, the Vineyard movement, and the emerging church. However, I found it more helpful (and efficient) to request that interviewees place JV on a "church map" in relation to the different branches of Christianity. Third, I asked respondents about their perception of JV's "central question". I then chose to ask JVers about Lawton's commonly used phrase "alternative basis for living" when describing the nature of the gospel. While he makes frequent use of several phrases in his Sunday talks, formal documents, and casual scenarios, I highlighted this particular one because it struck me as: (1) incredibly weighted with meaning, (2) an atypical cliché, and (3) a theological pivot point. Finally, I concluded the interview by requesting interviewees to compare the use of power (defined and illustrated as the currency of relational transactions) in JV versus the use thereof in other settings, such as the business arena or other friendship circles.

Results of Semi-structured Interviews

I will begin with some basic demographic information about the respondents. The 26 interviewees ranged in age from 22–65 with a mean age of 39, 14 were male and 12 were female; eight were single, 16 were married, one was divorced, and another widowed. The respondents combined for a total of 109 years of attendance, an average of 4.2 years per respondent. This may sound minimal, but at the time of the interviewees, the church itself was only seven years old. The respondents indicated an average frequency of attendance of one to two times per week. All of the interviewees had church experiences prior to JV. Over half of the interviewees had significant interaction in pentecostal or charismatic churches, five came from Church of England congregations, three were former Baptists, one was from a Free church, and another was previously Catholic. Two respondents said that they were churched as a child but then reentered via Jacobsfield Vineyard. This profile aligns closely enough with the demographic survey recounted in the previous chapter to be considered valid. The slight difference in duration of attendance (4.2 years for interviewees versus 3.3 years for survey respondents) can readily be attributed to the fact that the survey was more likely to register responses from new or fleeting members (ones who stay for three to six months but leave); these attendees were not assimilated to the point that I was able to connect with them for an interview. In the following section, I have recorded the findings of those interviews and miscellaneous comments of clarification.

When respondents were asked about the factors influencing their initial involvement at JV, the spectrum of responses was quite diverse. Ten spoke of the invitation of a close friend, seven said they felt JV was less showy and/or more personalized, another seven indicated a non-judgmental atmosphere, and six each referred to Lawton's transparency and a major conflict in a previous church. Other responses manifested by one-fifth or less of the respondents included a desire to participate in a church planting venture, feeling welcome socially, geographically proximity, being previously unchurched and looking to reenter church, and buying into JV's vision for a place of experimentation and exploration. While there was no dominating motif which emerged from these answers, their stories provided me, the interviewer, with a narrative framework for better understanding the rest of their responses.

However, a theme did seem to emerge from the next question about needs being met by the church. Fourteen, over half, talked about social needs (for example, belonging to a "church family" or home group). Ten cited opportunities for meaningful service and another ten referred to JV's role in helping them find purpose for life, a role to play congruent with life's calling, and/or personal development and growth. Other significant responses were belonging to a church vision in which one strongly believes, space to be oneself, and the relevance of teaching in Sunday services. As a result, the theme of meaningful participation in community seemed to characterize my investigation into their fulfilled needs at JV. JVers continually manifested a priority on relationships with other church members as well as functionally serving in roles within the life of the church.

The following question about crises of faith was born from Lawton's insistence on the church as a place where Christians are rethinking spirituality. I initially assumed that the Christians in this local church would have had prior faith crises similar to Lawton's necessitating this rethinking process. Instead, 22 interviewees said they had never experienced any such crisis. Eight of that number said they had never had one at all, another eight said the only crisis they could identify were the minor "ups and downs" of spiritual life, and the remaining six said that had never questioned their faith, but did have a significant life crisis while at JV.

Lawton claims that one of the primary ways JV is exploring what it means to be Christian is through a rediscovery of ancient forms of Christianity, and this emphasis is reinforced by the observations of historical Christianity at Sunday services. However, only four interviewees expressed personal appreciation for them. Twelve did not prefer them, and another ten felt neutral about them. Yet all ten who manifested neutrality followed up their sentiment by noting that they can appreciate them on the basis that the reason behind the observances is explained. An additional six of those who did not prefer them articulated that the observances can be valuable for new Christians or the unchurched. As a general rule, the longer an interviewee had been exposed to church, the more resistance they showed to these elements; they seemed to find it hard to understand why JVers were being taught familiar things in unfamiliar or irrelevant ways. For newer Christians, it was more of an educational experience and/or, as one JVer with only a few years of previous church experience told me, "just part and parcel of what it means to be in church."

Worship, as the Sunday services demonstrate, is a central practice at JV and of the Vineyard Organization as a whole. Fourteen respondents expressed strong affection for the musical quality of JV's worship. Ten felt that it was too restrained or restricted by advocating a desire for more external expressions and/or a longer duration of worship times while six appreciated time to passively connect with God. Seven were of the opinion that worship was about more than music, and a couple voiced the sentiment that JV was myopically focused on one expression of worship. Due to the complexity of the aspect of worship at JV, it will be treated more fully later in "Worship as a Representative Dimension of the Forces of Emergence", found in the next chapter.

Regarding the use of the Bible at JV, only five JVers expressed that they had no problems with the use of Bible at JV. Fifteen articulated that they would like to see more of the Bible used while eight suggested a better mix between straight Bible readings and culturally relevant concepts and teachings; another eight expressed confusion at how to best use the Bible as a tool for discipleship. Five respondents felt that the lack of the Bible's use at JV is potentially harmful for new Christians. However, four said that despite an apparent lack of overt Bible teaching, Lawton's teachings are saturated with biblical truth. Although nearly a third wanted a stronger blend between concepts and Bible citations, none of the respondents offered much specificity as to how the Bible ought to be used. This lack of consensus will be treated later.

When asked about the role of "doubts and questions" (a common phrase used by Lawton in Sunday talks) at JV, respondents provided clues as to why so few JVers attested to a crisis of faith. Nearly 40 per cent highlighted the culture of acceptance created by openly making space for doubts and questions, and about 30 per cent said that it was a significant personal reason for attending. Nearly a quarter appreciated the sense of space for approaching leaders about church decisions or teaching. For JV congregants, permitting others (outsiders or insiders) to think, to doubt, and to explore beyond a common stock of answers created, in their opinion, a very effective climate of acceptance. Put simply, their acceptance of people was directly linked with their acceptance of people's right to doubt, question, or disagree with the Christian faith.

There are two salient points with respect to JVers' comments about "spiritual maturity". First, the respondents' typical association with emotional and relational maturity manifested an intriguing correlation between spirituality and the skills of effective living. Generally, respondents linked the same handful of people—typically middle-aged or elder members who exhibited a remarkable amount of wisdom and care regarding life decisions—to the phrase. Interestingly, these "spiritually mature" JVers were not regularly public figures in Sunday services; in fact, I probably would not have known much about them if they were not repeatedly spoken of as significant role models. Second, despite some recurrent themes, the wide variation of answers and generalized ambiguity of the responses indicated that JVers are still working out exactly what their idea of maturity is. Seventeen, nearly two-thirds of those interviewed, linked spiritual maturity with emotional and relational maturity (that is, self-knowledge, life skills, people skills, and so on). Ten noted that it had nothing to do with age, and nine directly linked it with an individual's "relationship to God". Other typical replies included being real or vulnerable, willingness to recognize that growth is never complete, and time-bred experience. Only three commented that it involved knowledge of the Bible. Some even commented on the evolution of spiritual maturity at JV, namely that JV does not "force" people to mature and that while the "messy spirituality" aspect of Lawton's teaching is helpful, JV need to move beyond it. Nonetheless, the generalized idea of emotional and relational maturity served as an effective starting point for understanding what later will be labeled JV's "Arena for Growth and Maturity".

When JVers were asked to place their church on a church map in relation to other denominational categories, not a single respondent claimed that JV was a Vineyard church. Instead, 21 respondents categorized it by use of differentiation. Eight claimed JV was mostly similar to the emerging church movement, seven said it was a melting pot of many kinds of churches, and six refused (sometimes adamantly) to classify it. While one said JV is definitely not an emerging church, two claimed JV can be likened to an evangelical church, one to an Anglican church, and another to a "young pioneer church". This was perhaps one of the most telling responses of the semi-structured interviews, shedding much light on JV's identity as a liminal group, to be explored later.

As respondents were given the chance to articulate a "central question" for JV, the theme of "relevance" began to emerge quite strongly. The term recurred in many other places throughout the interviews, but came to the forefront during this question. Sixteen claimed that the central question was how to do church in order to be relevant to their surrounding community. Six phrased it as connecting people relationally with the surrounding culture, and six also asserted that the Jacobsfield Furniture Project was a significant outworking of the church's central question. The majority of responses, therefore, reflected a dominantly external focus. Others felt that it was the challenge of living Christian values in individual lives, or integrating of both "spiritual" and "secular" elements into one's life. When JVers were asked to expand on their meaning of the word "relevance", they often listed such things as interesting, appealing, understandable, something that makes people want to get involved, addressing the needs and issues of today, natural, assimilated, or real.

Regarding Lawton's oft-used phrase "alternative basis for living", respondents mirrored his teaching on the subject very closely. Though three had never heard the phrase, 15 pointed out that it is about not living life according to values of the world such as consumerism or materialism. Six stressed that it was synonymous with "the gospel" or "putting God at the center". Five asserted that it was Lawton's central teaching. While interviewees were often capable of articulating the sort of lifestyle an "alternative basis for living" rejected, no interviewees offered detailed descriptions of what the Christian alternative to materialism or individualism actually looked like. I do not mean to negate their understanding of this concept, but only to suggest that it reflects their larger trait of being in the transition between defining what Christianity is *not* and discovering what it may be.

To put the question about power at JV into context, at the time of the semi-structured interviews, JV as a community were being made aware of the leadership's plans to start an expansion congregation in a nearby town. It appeared that JVers were beginning to recognize that for JV to grow numerically, the JV universe—for seven years orbiting around Lawton—was in need of a step of decentralization. At the same time, the increased size of JV also made it more obvious that a large amount of influence was vested in Lawton. Some respondents appreciated this and the focus it brought to JV's collective direction; others felt rather uncomfortable with it. Nine interviewees emphasized Lawton's central authority role in a JV hierarchy, and many expressed need for greater accountability and/or balance to Lawton's power. However, others suggested that what legitimates Lawton's authority is trust gained via his transparency and character, and some asserted that all leaders at JV do not pretend to be better than others. There was no consensus of opinion, but the responses did underscore the centrality of Lawton's role at JV, for better or for worse.

Who Do JV Think They Are (Becoming)?

It is first of all important to expound upon the curious title of this section: "Who Do JV Think They Are (Becoming)?" There seemed to be both a widely held claim and the shared belief that JVers are on a journey, a pursuit of something they have not yet reached. In fact, it seemed that even their idea of who they should be was also under constant revision and questioning. Consequently, the life of JV cannot be viewed as a static reality; hence, analyzing it like a still-shot photo would be a betrayal of its nature. However, solely examining their ideals and aspirations would also be unfruitful and likewise ill-advised; thus understanding where they presently are on this journey into the future is a necessary task. This section's goal is to reflect upon where they have been, who they are striving to be, who they seem to be at present, and how these interact with one another (that is, how they are changing).

Drawing from the semi-structured interviews, other informal interviews, and participant observation data, I generated a framework of members' identity-claims by which to more deeply grasp JV's self-understanding. It was at this point in the research that I first made use of the sociological techniques of progressive focusing. Pooling all the data gained from conversations with, observations of, and specific identity-claims by JVers, I sought to group and classify them in order to discover common motifs which emerged from the data itself. I quickly ascertained that JVers continually characterized themselves around these four themes:

- Safety through honesty and openness
- Experimentation, particularly in communication with culture
- Maturity
- An uneasy relationship with evangelicalism

However, these four themes represented uniformly alongside each other did not seem to represent the full picture. After considering what the relationships between these themes might entail, it was concluded that there existed a relatively equal-plane relationship between the first three, but a unique difference given to the fourth theme regarding JV's relationship to evangelicalism. The other three motifs seemed to directly contrast with evangelicalism and find it as their point of reference/departure; hence, I have organized the following sections to reflect that relationship.

The JV Relationship to Evangelicalism

This section will focus on evangelicalism as JV's point of reference/departure. While acknowledging the difficulties of quantifying evangelicalism, it seemed that Webber's broad classification of evangelical strands would reflect the sentiments of JVers rather closely. Therefore, when citing the term "evangelicalism", this thesis will be making reference to the institutions, forms, and worldviews of the traditional and pragmatic evangelicals. JV's uneasy relationship with evangelicalism will be treated in three parts: JV's identity of different-ness, the process of sifting and discerning, and the dynamic of dual emergence.

An Identity of Different-ness

In the first phase of the fieldwork, I decided to explore their congregational identity by inquiring via informal interviews about their stance toward the "emerging church". I discovered that whereas most JVers see it as a very positive emphasis of Lawton's thinking, there is little consensus as to how much influence it has (or should have) at JV:

> "I've been reading *The Emerging Church* by Dan Kimball. I'm new to it, but I think the emerging church just comes down to people getting serious about doing church in a real way. For me, the furniture project has been huge because it's forced me get out of my comfort zone. It was scary at first, but I think serving poor people is something Jesus would do."

> "I think JV is 'emerging' because it's exploring the use of old liturgies and creeds … They're really meaningful to me."

> "An emerging church is one that is trying to figure out how to do and be church in a relevant way without having to be held back by the baggage of evangelicalism … but it gets a bit hyped-up to be honest … It's basically just a bunch of guys from different churches writing emails to each other … but it's good to be part of something bigger, not just an isolated place."

> "For me, it's the ability to ask questions and not have to have the answers … It's back to grace, … not dealing with people as a Christian machine."

> "The emerging church is Matt's hobby, project, and special interest. He is a communicative person and always into the new and trendy, so the emerging church is just Matt's latest interest. Post-modernism is good for Matt because it helps him grow, so it's good for JV as a result. Post-modernism especially helps Matt to communicate better, like using 'The Message' translation of the Bible. JV is doing what the emerging church says to do, but he would be doing that anyhow. JV is only held back by finance, not by imagination. Because Matt's always been into the latest stuff, Emergent [Village] gives him an arena in which to discuss stuff."

> "Here's my opinion of 'emerging church': Basically, what's happened is that the church has discovered that it's ten years behind everybody else and now it's trying to play catch-up in everything, including life skills."

> "We're struggling to find our place in being an emerging church while holding onto our own spirituality … I really enjoy taking post-modernity and banging the standard evangelism model on its head, but at the end of the day, I don't see what difference it makes … What difference does it make? It's still all about making disciples, and that's what I've been doing for years!"

Such a wide diversity of opinion as this precluded me from basing the JV identity solely on the emerging church movement. The dissimilarity in members' perspectives versus those of Lawton, as manifested in his own identity-claims, could be attributed to Lawton's formal training and extensive immersion in church resources, thinkers, and conversations of all varieties. His language when communicating the central issues of JV is therefore bound to be of a different genre than the language of members.

Since those initial findings proved relatively inconclusive, I decided to refashion the question for the semi-structured interviews and ask interviewees to place JV on a church map in relation to other strands of church. Although the question also returned a wide spectrum of answers, I believe they expressed a very similar sentiment. JVers often showed strong hesitation at pigeonholing JV into one particular category; the top three responses to this question, "Mostly similar to emerging church movement", "Melting pot of all", and "Unable to classify" accounted for over 70 per cent of total responses, indicating a thoroughly prevalent identity of "different-ness". One JVer, for example, told me that "JV is more 'an evolving church'—it's all in its own ecosystem." To accentuate the differentiation, not a single respondent linked JV with the Vineyard movement and nearly all felt themselves as distinguished from evangelicalism; of the remaining responses, only four saw JV as standing within a characteristically modern tradition. Nearly all respondents showed significant hesitation at classifying JV (some directly refused to pigeonhole JV in any way), and consistently cast their communal identity in light of their understanding of JV as a changing church. While a handful said JV was a "pick and mix" conglomeration of many different styles, even those who labeled JV "an emerging church" did so on a very different understanding of "emerging" from the concepts which I think its spokesmen would hold. Essentially, "emerging" for these interviewees simply meant that JVers were, to recount some frequently mentioned comments, growing numerically, trying new ideas, changing to meet the needs of their community, experiencing a constant level of change, or, as one respondent said, exhibiting the mentality of "always … progressing to do things better". While some did mention the influence of Emergent Village, the basis for their self-understandings of [non-] relation to other churches was always on the basis of their culture of change and mutation, though they rarely view themselves as a "research and development project" for the emerging church in the same way that Lawton does.

Sifting and Discerning

Therefore, it is necessary to first understand that JVers manifested quite a broad spectrum of attitudinal differences toward evangelicalism. This sentiment did not turn up solely in any one isolated question in the semi-structured interviews or other forms of data, but emerged as both a tangible and intangible element in their stories and other responses on a regular basis. For those with little or no church background, this relationship with evangelicalism was one of irrelevance and disinterest, as one JVer shared: "I never was a church girl—if you come from the outside, Christian culture is really quite laughable." For those JVers with thoroughly churched backgrounds (over 80 per cent according to the demographic survey), the relationship becomes more problematic. What I often heard was an eagerness to move beyond it, a need for a safe place to be healed from it, or a discontent with the habits learned from it, but simultaneously a hesitation to break all ties with it. There was a certain carefulness to not completely abandon their Christian heritage. One JVer explained: "A lot of people [in JV] have grown up in traditional churches, and they want to be different but don't want to throw everything out." For these JVers, the identity crisis does not revolve around questions such as "What does an emerging church look like and how does it function?" but, as one founding member told me, "we're trying to find a balance between rejecting what we've been taught in the past without rejecting everything … [We're] trying to figure out what understandings to hold onto and which ones to reject, specifically those of evangelicalism."

The JV dilemma may be summarized as such. On one hand, JVers desire to remain Christian, albeit according to a different criteria than their religious parentage has given them. On the other hand, they do not wish to move too far away from the evangelical tradition as it may feel that they are ceasing to be Christian. One member of the Eldership expressed to me that "we need to demystify the fundamentals of church, but we mustn't undermine them."

Two examples seem pertinent. One of the groups/ministries of JV is called "Cinema Trips" in which members attend a film and then meet afterwards to discuss it. When Mel Gibson's *The Passion of Christ*[2] came to cinemas, about 40 JVers attended a viewing and some then met afterwards at the Church Centre to reflect upon it as a group. Couches and chairs were arranged in a giant circle, snacks were available, no formal leadership was present, and 24 JVers of all age ranges sat down to share their thoughts on the movie. Most notable was the fervent disdain for a group of Christians from another local church who distributed evangelistic tracts (outlining steps to conversion) to viewers as they exited the theatre. However, even though JVers articulated disapproval over the distribution of tracts, they were still rather convinced of the thoroughly evangelical approach to Jesus' death (that is, the substitutionary atonement theory in which Christ died to compensate, or atone, for humanity's sins), even though pleas for conversion on this basis were never made in Sunday services. This commitment was manifested in sporadic recurring responses such as:

> "It's amazing that he did all that for me, and went through so much pain to save me."
>
> "[The film] helps you get a better picture of what it was really like for him to die on the cross. You hear about it, but until you see it, you don't realize how much pain he suffered so we could have eternal life."
>
> "I thought [during the film], 'Why did he have to go through so much pain?' And then I realized: it was the sin. The sin of the whole world was so bad. It was just so much."

Near the conclusion of the evening, one JVer commented: "It just made me think, 'How can I ever be the same?'" The group paused and nodded in agreement, but no one offered any specific reflections on what that might mean until one JVer commented, "Yes, as in, 'How can I not sacrifice when he has sacrificed so much?'" This seemed satisfactory to the group, and after another pause, the conversation moved on to other topics.

---

2 See Burnham (2004) for an academic treatment of the film.

One midweek evening, the home group in which I was involved gathered to discuss the subject of relationships. The home group leader had asked Lawton to take part in the evening to provide, in his view, a more seasoned perspective, and very quickly the discussion turned to sexual ethics. The dichotomy was almost visible—either participants had very little or no experience of sex whatsoever, or were trying to cope with the consequences of living with few sexual boundaries. Lawton offered no rules or strict guidelines; instead, he shared his own opinions on the matter, opinions which were often preceded by statements such as "I can't say that it's always wrong to" instead of precursors like "It's never right to". His primary emphasis seemed to be that many of the evangelical rules were not as static and universal as they attempt to be; therefore, an individual should decide what sort of place and significance they desire sex to have in their life and then make decisions from that context of meaning. The following week the home group leader took the group to the home of two JV elders for teaching on the same subject. This longtime JV couple, both from a more evangelical-Vineyard background, offered a somewhat different perspective on the subject of sexual ethics. Though unable to attend myself, I received very positive feedback from some participants at that meeting concerning the specificity of the suggestions given for adopting and maintaining definite rules of relational conduct for oneself. On a later occasion, I asked this JV elder (the husband) about the meeting. "What we're finding," he replied, "is that people want boundaries. Sure, they want to reposition or move the traditional ones, but they don't want the absence of boundaries." Such scenarios point to a dynamic of sifting and discerning occurring at JV related to doctrine, ethics, and their location in the worlds of church and culture.

Dual Emergence

Jamieson describes evangelical, pentecostal, and charismatic (EPC) churches as a significant stream of the Christian church. For perspective's sake, Peter Brierley's (2003) research claims that 35.8 per cent of Christians in the UK (2000 figure) belong to evangelical/pentecostal/charismatic churches. While "EPC churches are growing rapidly," Jamieson (2002, p. 11) comments, "it appears, at least in the West, that these same churches also have a wide-open back door through which the disgruntled, disillusioned, and disaffiliated leave." If this is true, then EPC churches are frequently the final stop on many Christians' journey out of church. Therefore, it is important to consider the question, "Are JV an EPC church?" On paper, a church organizationally identified with the Vineyard movement would undoubtedly be so; in numerous ways, the Vineyard organization is a theological hybrid between mainstream evangelical theology and pentecostal theology, and the movement has always been proud of its charismatic emphasis. Programmatically, JV do not differ much—if at all—from their Vineyard parents, and I found a significant number of JVers who articulated their faiths in ways identical to how Jamieson portrays EPC believers. At times, I wanted to categorize them with the EPC churches Jamieson describes; however, I hesitated at doing so. The sorts of leavers Jamieson depicts (with the exception of Disillusioned Followers) were still heavily involved and maturing their faith in intra-church ways at JV. Additionally, JV's operative theology was not always typical of EPC churches; while the absence of Christian clichés and packaged answers was noticeably significant, I found JVers to be tolerant of a wide variety of theological positions. It could be said that JVers had different beliefs about beliefs. Though JVers did not manifest contempt for or hesitancy toward doctrine, for them, believing the "correct" things was not a major issue.

This attitude coincides well with Jamieson's (2002, p. 161) use of the term "liminal groups"[3] who "are often aware of the greater societal rejection of the meta-narrative approach to life. They either consciously or intuitively realize that truth is multidimensional, paradoxical, and connected to both its historical and emerging representations." However, it would also be difficult to completely differentiate JV from the EPC vein of churches, primarily because they are its offspring and bear resemblance to it despite their journey of emergence from it; specifically, as I will later argue in the section "Worship as a Representative Dimension of the Forces of Emergence", JVers have inherited many of their aesthetic norms and a strong ethic of consistently reorienting their practices, characteristics which are very typical of EPC and pragmatic evangelical churches.

In order to portray a fuller understanding of the tricky relationship between JV and EPC churches, it is first necessary to view their identity-claims concerning their stance toward culture. JVers see themselves as emerging from culture in much the same way as they are emerging from evangelicalism. One JVer aptly remarked that:

> the twenty-somethings really make up the large part of JV. This age group is definitely a seeking age, especially for those who are single. JV values being yourself, and since many young people in our church have emerged from church contexts in which discipleship was a homogenous thing, an underlying theme seems to be compromise: How do I become the Christian God wants me to be and still be who I am? It's sort of an identity crisis related to being a Christian without being totally different. There is a certain element of coping with change, like we talk about the idea of journey. A lot of these twenty-somethings come from backgrounds with many secular influences and friends. Therefore, I think [the central question] is building into oneself those influences to become a good Christian without completely abandoning these other forces.

JVers often viewed culture as full of well-meaning wanderers, yet this creates a certain tension: since culture (or in this case, "the Other") is not perceived as inherently evil, there is a willingness to identify with the Other in practice, but alongside this is a parallel desire to be other-worldly while not being anti-worldly,

---

3 The notion of liminality can best be seen in the work of Victor Turner. A summary of this concept and its potential pertinence for the emerging church can be found in Chapter 5.

as one JVer said: "[W]e don't want to end up as a ghetto with our own language, morals, and quirks the rest of the world cares nothing about."

A contrast with Webber's categories of traditional and pragmatic evangelicalism may be appropriate at this point. Traditional evangelicals built their cause on separation from the world, with only minimal identification. The pragmatic evangelicals (the Vineyard movement included) sought to bridge the relevance gap which their traditionalist parents had created by making Christianity accessible to the unchurched. However, as Webber argues, the pragmatic evangelicals adopted a consumerized Christian message which was accessible, but not powerful. JVers want to find a new identity which shares ground with both culture and evangelicalism, but does not identify wholly with either. Therefore, it is in this context—a "reconstruction site"—of an uncertain emergence from evangelicalism and secular culture in which JVers set themselves.

Safety through Honesty and Openness

The themes of "doubting", "questioning", "honesty", and "openness" were cited by interviewees far more than terms such as "evangelical" or "evangelicalism"; however, I chose to classify the relationship with evangelicalism first because this need for permission to question and be transparent was born from prior church experiences. To put this theme in proper perspective, one can consider why and how most members joined JV. Though Lawton claims that 60 per cent of JVers are previously unchurched, the demographic survey and interviews indicated that nearly all have some form of church background, albeit very limited in some cases. What Jacobsfield Vineyard did offer, in congregants' eyes, was a safer church culture in which to question, recover, and mature. The catalyst for experiencing this culture of "safety through honesty and openness" was repeatedly attested to be: (1) loving relationships with others who accept them as they are and (2) Lawton's transparent leadership.

Relational Acceptance

First, a relational atmosphere precipitated this sense of openness. Very few congregants joined JV because they were an "emerging church", an experimental church, or a trendy church; rather, most JVers joined and stayed because they felt the church was a place to authentically belong as themselves with all their doubts, weaknesses, and problems. Indeed, all four of the top responses in the semi-structured interviews given for initial involvement at JV corresponded with a relational dynamic, and the chief response for needs met by JV—articulated by over half the respondents—was social in nature, a sense of belonging. Even a relative newcomer noted that "[i]t's more open here. I don't know how to explain it, I just feel like it's more open to stuff." During my fieldwork, I regularly heard the following diagram repeated to me, often in emphatic fashion, as JVers described their approach toward evangelism. These JVers would draw (either conceptually or literally) two rows of three train carriages each. On the first line they would label the carriages in the order "BELIEVE, DO, FEEL", explaining that Christianity generally says that first one must believe Christian things, then one must do them, and finally one will feel like a Christian. On the second train, they reversed the order to reflect their preferred model: "FEEL, DO, BELIEVE". Generally, they would then say that their mission was to help people belong so eventually they could believe, but belief was not necessary at first.

Congregants communicated a strong sense of pride about the space JV created for people at all stages of their spiritual journey. "The thing with JV is," one JVer told me in an interview, "and this works and it [sometimes] doesn't work—if you want to take God seriously, that's great and if not, that's OK too …. At some churches, it's not OK, but JV gives you space to explore where you're at." Another JVer told me (via email), "I suppose my questions on church growth are not for growth sake, but rather *not* inhibiting growth. I feel that Church growth is part of our DNA, in terms of growing God's Kingdom and allowing as many people to connect as possible. I guess I don't want to be part of a 'trendy' church, just part of a healthy growing community." Though JV valued the addition of members, they were extremely hesitant to intentionally recruit for the sake of becoming a larger congregation.

This relational atmosphere was also articulated through the vernacular of "realness". This term—"real"—recurred consistently in discourse with JVers, each time in reference to a relational dimension. For some, being real entailed becoming "part of the communication web" of the surrounding community, for others it was linked with messy spirituality, and to others "realness" spoke of people being who they are, caring for each other and meaning it, having no pretenses, not being perfect, but trying to "do the Sunday life throughout the week"; in any case, it involved an element of knowing others in extra-superficial ways. "We all have different hang-ups," a JVer told me, "so one person's struggle may not be another's, and JV is a safe place to have hang-ups and work through them. It's OK here to have dirty washing." Another JVer appreciated the fact that at JV one's values do not have to correspond with others in order to belong which, in his opinion, goes against the grain of other churches which fear "corruption" from people who are different.

Lawton's Leadership

Lawton's style of leadership and teaching seemed to be the very catalyst for the environment of relational safety. JVers frequently spoke of their appreciation for Lawton's honesty about his own struggles, so much that it would difficult to underestimate its significance. One such interviewee spoke of Lawton's honesty, particularly concerning his family situation, and the way in which it "sets the model" for the rest of JV. "From the very beginning," one founding member told me, "Matt made it very clear that JV would be a place where honesty would be a high priority." During Lawton's crisis, this value became even more solidified in the JV culture: "As a result of Matt's openness during his crisis, the church is full of people with problems." One interviewee who attested to a crisis of faith noted that Lawton's transparency about his own crisis "paved the way" for her own, adding that "it's almost as if Matt had to go through that [crisis] to allow others to as well."

However, while Lawton's transparency is to be acknowledged as a significant influence upon the JV culture, the fuller treatment of how leadership is used at JV must be provided. In the semi-structured interviews, the question pertaining to the use of power at JV frequently revealed three major attitudes toward leadership at JV: (1) Lawton uses power more responsibly than many other leaders whom the interviewees' encounter in other circles, (2) JVers are not very democratic due to the large amount of power Lawton holds, and (3) JVers are relieved that the elders and trustees are in place to (theoretically) balance his power if he tried to use it improperly. One JVer summed up the scenario well:

> [Power] is a big issue, and might be a bigger one. There is an interest in balancing the power at JV because it's led by a big person with a big personality … It was and is essential in making the church happen, but as the church grows, the dynamics will change and Matt will need to balance his power … This hasn't happened that much despite efforts to spread it out [via the elders and trustees]. Matt doesn't exhibit an unwillingness to spread it out, but it's never happened before, so no one knows what will happen if measures are made to balance things.

At JV the culture of leadership is shaped by a number of forces. The Vineyard movement, the initial fashioner of JV's culture, has a strong tradition of apostolic-style leadership—that is, leaders vested with full control of the church's decisions. While Vineyard churches have some procedures in place for dealing with deviance in very extreme cases, for the most part, the Vineyard organization trusts these individuals (or, in many cases, married couples) with full authority over their respective congregations. As one JVer with a long history in the Vineyard movement explained, "In many ways, it is like a small dictatorship." To an arguably slightly lesser extent, JV inherited this model and continued it through their early years; Lawton and his wife had the final authority on every matter of church life. Despite the addition of the Eldership (for spiritual oversight) and the Trustees (for organizational oversight) in the past few years (prompted particularly by Lawton's breakdown), JV have remained a leader-centered church in many respects, or as another JVer noted, "a one man band". While there is a notable amount of responsibility shared by these volunteer leaders, JVers feel that the strength of Lawton's influence has continued; if anything, it has grown significantly over the years.

However, observations of the Sunday services did not reveal an overwhelming presence of Lawton; while he generally hosted the service and gave the sermon, he played little or no part in the 30 minutes of worship or the ancient-future faith elements, habitually shared responsibility with others for sharing notices, regularly opened the microphone for various JVers to share words or pictures of encouragement and spiritual insight for the congregation, and let others lead and distribute the monthly practice of communion. Decentralization was even more common outside of Sundays: home groups were relatively autonomous, ministries were coordinated by lay leaders, and social functions were consistently executed by volunteers. On the other hand, many JVers expressed the sentiment that Lawton has a tendency to become a "control freak" when he gets stressed, a fault which he readily and openly admits.

It could be said, then, that the leadership challenge for JV is how to match the increasing demands of a growing congregation and the presence of a strong central figure who has strongly led the church since its birth with an increased atmosphere of accountability and shared authority. While Lawton's perceived use of power provoked diverse and sometimes negative opinions amongst JVers, many, if not all, would agree that Lawton's own transparency, particularly in his Sunday talks, sponsored and gave permission to the free expression of members' doubts, weaknesses, and struggles.

Space for Being Real

The link between honesty/openness and safety is important to understanding the culture of JV. To many JVers, feeling free to be who they are—especially with their weaknesses—is the quality which makes JV different from other churches, and becomes the starting point for their development. "If there's one word to describe JV," one interviewee told me, "it's 'real' … You can't possibly go through anything in life without having doubts, otherwise you're just fooling yourself. At JV we're just normal people trying to figure life out." As stated earlier, permitting doubts and questions played a complex role. On one hand, it was a core value—JVers continually attested to the need for respecting others' right to be uncertain, to question even the most basic claims of truth, to doubt anything they chose. Yet on the other hand, there was a small amount of overt "doubting" occurring amongst congregants. When the semi-structured interviewees were asked about crises of faith, only four identified a time when they endured a season of doubting the Christian faith, questioning the meaning of life, or some other parallel faith crisis to that of Lawton.

How then can something be of such enormous value to JVers and yet not be interwoven with their personal histories? As the fieldwork period progressed, it became clear that JV's acceptance of doubt was directly linked with their acceptance of people. For instance, one twenty-something JVer emphatically told me that the first time she had ever heard someone say it was permissible to have doubts about one's faith was when an elder gave a Sunday morning talk in her early months at JV in which "he said that it was OK to doubt. I was so overwhelmed. I'm allowed to doubt! And that doesn't mean I'm not a Christian!" Another twenty-something interviewee commented that JV's acceptance of doubts is:

> stronger than any other church I've ever been in … At JV, it's almost expected that people have doubts and questions … Other churches imply doubts mar one's

> character and indicate a weak faith. [JV's acceptance of doubts and questions] helps people feel accepted. It creates a culture of acceptance … Everyone has small [doubts], and since big ones [at JV] are OK, small ones don't become big ones. Because at most churches, small ones aren't accepted and then they turn into big ones.

Another expressed that allowing uncertainty is "very liberating, especially because other churches in my past gave the impression that you have to have apologetic answers in your hip pocket … I like the ability to say 'I don't know' and for that to be OK, especially because things don't always work out in ways we expect, and it should be OK to step back and say, 'I don't know why God did that.'" Safety for doubting, holistic acceptance, and "being real" were, for JVers, inseparable.

Furthermore, this culture of safety was the prerequisite for the maturity which they sought, as one JVer indicated to me: "We're all different, with different theologies, at all different stages of our journeys of trying to work things out … You don't have to come as a pre-packaged squeaky clean person." As the following section will demonstrate, while members had quite an intentional view of growth, the conceptual clarity of that maturity is still in embryonic form.

Arena for Growth and Maturity (Though We're Not Sure What That Is)

In many venues in addition to the "spiritual maturity" question in the semi-structured interviews, growth was also rather central to their self-identity. The following section will demonstrate that while there is: (1) an implicit expectation for maturity at JV, there is also (2) a very individual orientation to it, (3) a wide diversity of definition concerning it, and (4) no consensus on the resources for achieving it.

An Expectation for Individuals

As one JVer explained, JV have the philosophy of "come as you are, but you can't stay as you are." Another told me, "At JV, there is a tremendous emphasis on getting our lives right … Church should be a constant process of changing people, and that's a painful process." Although maturity was an implicit part of involvement in the JV community, growth had a very individual orientation to it. While many interviewees articulated maturity as legitimated by things such as increased relational skills, the responsibility and incubator for this growth was nearly always communicated as an individual one. One interview couple, for instance, assessed JV's effectiveness in breeding spiritual maturity. While the husband noted that it was "happening OK" at JV, the wife expressed some hesitation: "I don't know if it's happening, but I'm not sure that it's our business to know. People mature as much as they want to, and everyone grows at different paces …." She then said that JVers are maturing people "as much as any church is, [especially by] giving people an opportunity to grow as much as they want to." Therefore, on one hand, JV have a "tremendous emphasis on getting [their] lives right" and, on the other hand, they value a nonjudgmental, individual-based "messy spirituality". These two dyanmics have created an eagerness to discover what Christian maturity, for them, ought to be.

Various Definitions

In the semi-structured interviews, two-thirds of respondents defined "spiritual maturity" at JV as emotional and relational maturity, and the next most common sentiment—that spiritual maturity has nothing to do with age—was expressed by nearly 40 per cent of interviewees. Though a third acknowledged that it is linked to one's "relationship with God", less than a tenth mentioned such things as Bible knowledge or the exercise of spiritual gifts. "Spiritual" acts such as prayer, exuberant worship, or supposed authority over evil forces of a supernatural dimension were apparently of no special importance to JVers; rather, they saw maturing as not so much a process of conforming to biblical standards, but a ripening into a more effective adulthood. For JVers, maturity in a general sense was nearly indistinguishable from spiritual maturity. This maturity was expressed via such things as increased self-responsibility, clearer direction, better relationship skills, and the acquisition of tools to deal with the everyday problems of life. Spirituality was wrapped up in these "secular" aspects of life, and any "spiritual" habit which did not directly improve the former was considered essentially futile, sometimes emphatically rejected altogether. One JVer commented on the relationship between Lawton's crisis, spiritual growth, and life development: "Because of Matt's background, he was forced to grow up, and this as much a spiritual thing as anything. Matt's learned to express power in adult ways … This church isn't about theology, it's about growing up in a way that most people never have. What allowed [Lawton] to do that was post-modernity."

A return to Jamieson will help to locate JV on the map of maturity-development. It is be my assertion that JV represent rather closely what Jamieson (2002, p. 159) calls "liminal churches". "Whereas the marginal group[4] is primarily focused on the past which they have left and is continuing to make sense of their leaving, the liminal group is primarily focused on what lies in the future. In faith terms it is looking to develop, build and nurture an ongoing faith." He (pp. 158–9) indicates that these liminal churches are in an "in-between time" which becomes the "threshold of the new." Despite the fact that most JVers are open about their previous frustrations in churches, I found not a single JVer who manifested traits of an angry Disillusioned Follower. He (p. 159) continues, "Groups with a core of Disillusioned Followers and Reflective Exiles are typically marginally focused … Some groups—often those made up of church leavers who have been outside of church for some time and with strong Transitional Explorers and Integrated

[4] Jamieson defines marginal groups as those which tend to focus on what they have left. They are eager to deconstruct previous beliefs and understandings, and their uniting feature is a previous common experience which has now passed but is nevertheless significant for their sense of identity.

Wayfinders—are predominantly liminal in focus." Though Jamieson does not explore this issue specifically, it does not seem possible to have a church entirely composed of Transitional Explorers and Integrated Wayfinders. The maturity of a church is be measured by the aggregate of Christians in the later stages of faith development but rather by the quality of the relationship between those in later stages and the stage two and three Christians. As one JVer (who had also read Jamieson's book) said, "It's not that [at JV] we don't have stage three Christians, but that the stage three-ers don't crucify those who are in stage four and beyond."

The heterogeneity, then, is apparent. While friction may not occur between members, for those concerned with JV's processes of assimilation and socialization of new members, it is more problematic. One JV elder explained to me that a central concern of hers is "How do we disciple people in the context of the informal, post-modern church we're trying to be? … What's next? What are we going to do with these people who are coming in?"

Resources for Developing Maturity

One JVer immediately responded to the question about spiritual maturity at JV by saying, "At JV, I don't think we've worked out how to bring people to spiritual maturity." She continued by commenting that "all the theory about discipleship is encompassed at JV, but some sections of JV are really growing and others aren't … it's very experimental … I'm not sure we've got the right processes in place." Two examples—the use of the Bible and observances of historical Christianity—illustrate their dilemma of utilizing resources for fostering maturity or growth.

First, the use of the Bible presented itself as a challenge for JVers. As I will demonstrate, two factors seemed to be at work. First, due to a large number of new and young Christians, JVers typically had a limited knowledge of the Bible. Many of the older members of JV whom I interviewed manifested a common concern: they emphasized the need for the Bible to play a role in spiritual formation, but were hesitant about educating others in the same fashion in which they were taught. Some interviewees used expressions such as "guilt trips" or "learning it parrot fashion". One elder JVer summarized the dilemma well:

> I'm not sure that we're cultivating a reliance on the Bible, but that's my experience, and I can't say that it's right for everyone or that everyone needs it in the same way … I don't expect them to have to go through the traditional grounding in the Bible like I did, but there's still a gap there, and I'm not sure how it should be bridged. Traditional teaching doesn't work, but I'm not sure what does! … There are so many voices in culture saying 'This is truth!', so what are you standing on that makes you different?

In JVers' reflections on the role of the Bible at JV, they never manifested doubt that the church was making "biblical" decisions or conveying "biblical" doctrine, but they did indicate a desire for Lawton to back up his teachings with more of the Bible (nearly 60 per cent in the semi-structured interviews articulated a desire for the Bible to be used more often). JVers often spoke of (indirectly and sometimes directly) the Bible and cultural relevance being opposites of one another, saying that they would like to see more of a "mix" between the two.

Second, Scripture seemed like a logical component of discipleship, though traditional methods of educating Christians about the Bible seemed inappropriate.  At JV, Lawton articulated Scripture as the Christian's "family history" and sometimes referred to his desire for the books of the Bible to be divided up into separate entities organized by genre: when one would like to read biblical poetry, one could reach for the Psalms, or when one wanted to study Jewish history, one could reach for Judges or II Kings, and so on. He referred to Bible characters as people comparable to us—with similar faults and weaknesses—who were trying to "work out" what God wanted them to do, sometimes succeeding and other times failing. One member commented to me that "people sometimes miss the use of the Bible [at JV] because they think it should be difficult, and it's not … Matt uses small parts and gives it in digestible servings, but the congregation finds it hard to accept this because they don't feel as if they've been hit hard enough." JVers newer to the Christian faith seem to find Lawton's teachings on Scriptures rather logical and easy to assimilate, while it appeared from interview responses that those with a longer history in evangelical churches typically had trouble with them.

Despite their liminal identity, JVers still wanted the Bible to play a prominent role in their church and their individual lives. Though they are discarding many typical presuppositions and extremes of doing church, they have discarded a need for legitimating their practices. For this, they desired much more than just the word of their pastor (despite the enormous amount of trust which they place in him); they needed a clear connection to the larger Christian tradition. However, many of the presuppositions which they have rejected (for example, "hard sell" Christianity, believing before belonging) have seemingly come from that heritage, resulting in a sometimes uncomfortable tension.

A second illustration relates to their use of practices of historical Christianity. Toward the end of the fieldwork, observances of the Christian calendar alongside their respective historical practice (for example, reading the Psalms of Ascent during "Ordinary Time", lighting candles for Candle Mass, ash on the forehead for Ash Wednesday, and so on) was not an infrequent occurrence in JV Sunday services. However, only a minority of JVers expressed a considerable degree of personal preference for these observances. Of the semi-structured interviewees, only four declared a strong affection for them; another ten showed appreciation for the explanation of the observance, though showed hesitation at praising the practice itself as helpful for themselves. The remaining respondents, nearly half, indicated that the observances did not benefit them personally, though half of this group was quick to endorse the value of the practices for new Christians or the unchurched. As a result, JVers were more discontent with the practical dimensions of the observances, not necessarily the purpose for the observances. It appeared that JVers shared, to a certain degree, an identity crisis of wanting to find roots in the past, but found it difficult to relate to the practical expressions of the past, as a sampling of their comments demonstrates:

> "They're not bothering me, but they're not doing anything for me … They link us back to the past, but I don't see a lot of relevance to them. Matt does explain [their significance], and that's good, but it doesn't mean much to me."
>
> "It's good because it's important to understand the importance of the Church and why certain things are practiced … But it needs to be done in a relevant way. We need to know why certain days are special, but we need to observe them differently than we've observed them in the last two thousand years. Like when we did Candle Mass where the [historical] church emphasized Jesus as the Light of the World by blessing the year's supply of candles. That didn't mean anything to me, so maybe we need to update things like that … We can't lose the message in the observance of whatever it is we're doing … We're very close to just following and meditating on the day itself instead of what the day means."
>
> "They came as quite a shock to me because it wasn't something I expected in a Vineyard church … But having thought about it, I can see the part it plays in building new believers and putting them into the right context … Now I realize it's good for me too."
>
> "JV uses them because they have meaning, not simply for tradition's sake … But we have to ask the question, 'Are these things going to connect with people around us?' And the answer I come up with is 'Probably not.'"
>
> "They are sufficient, but they haven't become the main thing, which is good … We don't observe these holy days and pray these prayers and drink from this cup because 'it's the holy day' or 'it's the prayer' or 'it's the cup', but because this is the day when this or that happened and it's worth remembering."
>
> "We can't forget where we came from, but at the same time, we can't get stuck in the past."
>
> "There is a relevant point to remembering them now. When we remember them, it's very easy to overlook the fact that originally they were relevant … But the question that you have to ask is 'Are those things relevant now?' Maybe you'll decide that the idea behind it is relevant, but the celebration itself is not."

JVers showed a strong understanding of the ultimate intent of these observances—the communication of Christian beliefs and connection/grounding in the past—but felt a hesitancy with the outworking of these aims.

Uncertainty about Maturity

"At JV," one interviewee told me, "there's a fluid sense of ideas, and there's no set formula for being a Christian." All these issues related to maturity reflect a dilemma which could be represented as such: "If not [practice or belief], then what? And why—on what basis?" While JVers were relieved that the Bible's teaching was not being imposed on members, there was a growing sense of discomfort that the Bible—a confusing but useful tool for spiritual growth (in their minds)—was not being utilized to its full potential. Or, to illustrate further, if we value being nonjudgmental, then what does it mean to be accountable to others? If hard sell evangelism is alienating, then what is a Christian's responsibility regarding evangelism? If acceptance and inclusion is a hallmark of Christianity, then how should Christians view homosexuality? Whereas JV have carved out an "arena for maturity", they are still mildly uncertain as to what to place in this space. Thus, the re-fusion of these two horizons—life development and spirituality—in an environment of safety was enough for many JVers to consider JV a place to call home. However, many JVers also felt the need to identify themselves as an place of experimentation in order to better communicate with the surrounding culture.

Experimentation and Communication with Culture

The fourth theme which emerged from the congregational study was a common desire for experimentation and communication with culture, but with very differing levels of continuity. This aspect of their self-identity was in a state of mutation more than the others. There was no definite consensus of strategy, but the value they placed on it was significant.

JV's Raison D'être

For JVers, experimentation in doing church was not refashioning practices to satisfy personal tastes, but for the purpose of better communicating to the culture around them those beliefs and values which make up who they are. From this center of meaning was born their desire to do church in "relevant" ways, clearly expressed in responses to the semi-structured interview question regarding JV's central question. Over 60 per cent cited the challenge of doing church in an effort to be relevant to the neighboring community, and nearly a quarter spoke of connecting people relationally with the surrounding culture. Many respondents also pointed to the Furniture Project as an example of how JVers are attempting to answer this central question. Put simply, JVers framed their *raison d'être* almost exclusively with an external or outward-looking focus. "How do we connect with the local community by becoming part of it?" one asked. Many felt that connecting with outsiders should be a primary task, one that informs their practice: "How do we do a church that's relevant to today's culture's ways of thinking, lifestyle, ways of communicating, and that's relevant to people's lives?" Whereas their perceptions of maturity were quite varied, this motif of externally-focused relevance was potentially the most thorough and homogenous of all. Being "relevant" was a

shared value amongst congregants, but no consensus was present as to exactly what that meant with a great degree of specification. Some referred to playing worship tunes of a soft rock genre, others pointed to the casual atmosphere of Sunday services, while others felt that it was presenting the Christian message without the presence of religious language. The common denominator in all such discussions, however, was methods (of doing church) for the purpose of credibility with the unchurched.

While this may seem indicative of a pragmatic evangelical identity, JVers never voiced a need for new programs or ministries. What they did value was the accessibility of their own tradition to those outside of it. Church traditions themselves were not rejected or despised; what they did reject was feeling pressured to communicate those beliefs to their friends in what they saw as obnoxious ways. JVers did not feel that they were doing church in a "post-modern way" or in any definite strategy at all; in fact, they appeared to become slightly agitated at such suggestions. One interviewee even expressed that she was "anxious … and afraid that in all this eagerness to embrace post-modernism, we'll throw the baby out with the bath water." The following summarizes this attitude rather well:

> In the UK, [Christianity] is seen as boring, but people at JV have realized that it isn't and now want to show others it isn't, so our goal is finding ways to communicate that to people outside church. The evangelism movement emphasized trendy ways of reaching people, but people in our church have realized that those things don't work … It has something to do with spirituality because the evangelism era treated some spirituality as evil, but people were just trying to find answers. We're realizing people are into spirituality and we're all asking the same questions about spirituality and the meaning of life, and we want JV to say that you might find them where you don't expect them (in church).

Attitude toward Evangelism

As this quote illustrates and other findings confirm, if there is any one passionately held value with respect to modern evangelicalism, it is the rejection of their evangelistic techniques. One JVer, before leaving his childhood church as a teenager (JV, incidentally, was his first re-entry to Christianity since then), recounted to me his experience with his former church's trip to the 1989 Billy Graham Crusade: "I can still remember the title: 'L-I-F-E', in big bold letters, followed by 'Come and Hear the Man Who Can Make Sense of It'. I went and got nothing out of it … It was such a pointless event; it didn't talk about my life." He then narrated to me how, at his church's follow up meeting, he expressed his frustration with Graham's evangelism strategy to his fellow church members who, in his opinion, severely looked down on him for protesting. While this JVer emphasized the fact that he did not have a problem with Graham himself, what upset him most was the way in which the members of his church "weren't even open to the remotest possibility of there being anything wrong with [the crusade] … Evangelism has no set format!"

Another story may help to illustrate. During the *Passion of the Christ* film discussion mentioned earlier, while the violent nature of the film provoked much dialogue, there were a few topics which also fostered notable amounts of conversational energy, not least of which was their negative reaction to some evangelistic tracts handed out by another local church as viewers exited the theater. In fact, this was one of the first subjects mentioned: "What did you all think of those blue leaflets those people gave us at the end? What was the point of that?" one JVer remarked. The palm-sized tracts, entitled "How to be a Christian", explained the standard evangelical version of salvation, culminating in a sample prayer for reconciliation with God. His comment prompted the group to express a series of disapproving comments. Not a single JVer spoke in favor of these tracts, illustrated by comments such as:

> "That was the worst thing to follow up a film like that! I would rather them not to have been there."
>
> "[The tracts] weren't even nice. They were copied on cheap paper and looked tacky. It was awful, what a bad impression to give."
>
> "They're almost spoiling it. They're giving a completely wrong picture … The message of Christianity is about so much more than just 'pray this prayer'."
>
> "We should print up our own tracts to fix the damage the others do!"
>
> "I mean, if you were a non-Christian and you got one of those as you came out of the theater, what kind of impression would you get? After all that, and then you're told all [the film's message] means is saying some words!"

Scenarios such as this point to a series of conclusions about their attitude to evangelism: (1) They had a strong distaste for confrontational evangelistic techniques. (2) They still wanted to communicate "the message of Christianity". (3) What was still unclear was how then to communicate this message and exactly what that message is if it is more than praying a prayer for salvation in the afterlife.

Communicating with Their Culture

In light of Webber, JV have not been left unaffected by the cultural emphasis on "the medium is the message", a shift which he feels is at the heart of the post-modern turn. Webber (2002, p. 65) contends that the:

> idea that "the medium is the message" holds important ramifications for the communication of the Christian faith. First, the real message of Christianity is not rational propositions but the person of Jesus Christ with whom a personal relationship is possible. Second, this personal relationship is experienced and

> communicated in a community—the church, his body. Third, to communicate a relationship with Jesus Christ, the church must be an embodied presence, an authentic and real community in which the Spirit dwells. Fourth, the primary concern of the church is to communicate not dogma, though it does have its place, but faith. Fifth, the primary way of communicating faith is through a combination of oral, visual, and print forms of participatory immersed communication (or cultural transmission).

These points were very characteristic of JVers' worldviews. As stated earlier, JVers had "different beliefs about beliefs". Since many of them have experienced firsthand the unpleasant side of churches who insist on dogmatic propositional beliefs, they still find themselves equally as (if not more) eager to communicate the Christian faith. Nearly all with whom I spoke about the topic manifested a desire for "lifestyle evangelism" as opposed (and sometimes vehemently opposed) to a propositionally-based approach to evangelism. This shift of attitude bears resemblance to Webber's younger evangelicals; he (p. 70) claims that this group "who were born, reared, and educated within the new forms of communication and the postmodern world, more thoroughly embrace the implications of an embodied truth communicated through the cultural transmission of faith." While many JVers do come from this generation, their emphasis on communicating with culture in embodied fashion did not seem to be spawned directly from their immersion in new communicative technology (although that was undoubtedly widespread at JV), but their significant commitment to faith and a desire to maintain a relationship with their culture. Though JVers do not typically take responsibility for converting the unchurched, they do sense the need to communicate the Christian message in a clearer way to those around them.

Chapter 4
Identifying a Central Theological Question

Sensing a Central Question

What is one to make of these themes—emergence from evangelicalism, safety for "being real", Christian maturity, and communicating with culture? Does the JV congregational study lead to many disparate concerns or a single, essential issue? Is there a means of synthesizing them or ascertaining an underlying cause? How are their problems theological in nature? This chapter seeks to recount my own journey of thinking about JV's central question. As mentioned in Chapter 1, what lends this congregational study its practical theological orientation is the working towards a central theological question. Of course, there is no way to say objectively what a congregation's question is. The questions that seemed essential to me may not be of significance to another researcher, as they are shaped by my own history and interests. It must therefore be noted that a central question is ultimately labeled by the researcher, but is done in rigorous cooperation with the research findings and the members of the group being researched. Describing my own thinking explicitly, therefore, will aid the reader in reaching his/her own conclusions.

The journey to ascertain a central question began before I even entered Jacobsfield Vineyard. In my very first pre-fieldwork interactions with Lawton, he stressed to me the three questions which guide his own thinking: (1) what does it mean to be Christian? (2) what does it mean to be church? And a third, more personal one, (3) what does it mean to be a pastor? His leadership of Emergent Village UK and the venturesome spirit typical of church plants provoked a strong curiosity within me about how this might actually be manifested in the life of a local church. I approached JV expecting anything from a congregation full of enterprising church reformers to an inflexible church disinterested in their pastor's hobby-horse. During my first months of participant observation in JV, I felt there was little remarkable about the JV culture. The worship songs of the worship renewal movement, the programmatic resemblance to EPC churches, or their emphasis on praying for one another reminiscent of my pentecostal upbringing caused me to feel hesitant about the value of the study. Simply put, at times it was too familiar.

Simultaneously, I sensed a different worldview at work, a tolerance for ideological diversity, and an intriguing hermeneutic for interpreting the Christian life. While JVers often spoke of improving their practices for doing church, many also talked about shifts in thinking about church. There did seem to be some evidence that other JVers besides Lawton were also asking questions related to what it meant to be Christian and what it meant to be church. As one JVer told me, "We're challenging the idea that we've got to do something different to reach post-moderns … Our uniqueness lies in our desire to embody a new story." JV allowed me (and its adherents) to fully participate without the expectation of mirroring their propositional beliefs. I had expected to spend my time dissecting new forms of doing church (which at JV were relatively rare for a church community claiming to be an "emerging church"); sensing a more ideological differentiation from evangelical Christianity, the JV interpretive framework became a centerpiece of my exploration, particularly in analyzing the semi-structured interviews.

Fortunately, JVers themselves were often more keen to articulate questions than definitive answers. Their questions, as with my own, must be viewed as a product of their histories. As I listened to and reflected upon their stories, I ascertained that many JVers with whom I spoke were emerging from experiences in which they realized that either or both of the two worlds to which they commonly referred—evangelical strands of Christianity and post-Christian culture—were dissatisfying. Consequently, I concluded that the JV story seems to be one of dual emergence: JV are unified by their common frustration with both evangelical versions of Christianity and their surrounding culture and a common desire to develop an identity apart from them while not entirely disconnecting from them. This transformation of identity was not happening at a revolutionary speed, though, as I hoped before beginning the study; it was occurring, though, in a more evolutionary way. What was fairly certain from the framework of members' identity-claims were starting points such as safe space for transparency and weaknesses, a desire to unlearn unhelpful habits from evangelical Christianity, the need for Christian maturity, and the necessity of doing this in relevant ways to their surrounding community. What was uncertain, however, were the specifics of how to go about these tasks. Consequently, my journey toward a central theological question prompted me to think in terms of JV as a site of "tentative  reconstruction", and the more I spoke with JVers about that phrase, the more they indicated a resonance with it. There was emergence, the sources of which were clear while the destination was not.

Worship as a Representative Dimension of the Forces of Emergence

As I progressed toward Jacobsfield Vineyard's central practical theological question, I felt that a representative microcosm would be helpful for illustrating their transition of identity. As I considered which slice of JV would be most appropriate for illustrating this question, I continually returned to their corporate practice of worship as a case study of their central question. I chose their public practice of worship (as expressed in Sunday meetings) for several reasons:

- The entire congregation was affected by it.
- It was a regular tradition (30 minutes at the opening of every Sunday meeting).
- It was something valued by most JVers as a distinctive characteristic of JV.
- It was a largely unresolved area with a wide spectrum of opinions, many of which were very strong opinions.
- It was not a solely pastor-driven aspect of the church's existence.
- Since it was a communally shared experience under transition, its evolution (or lack thereof) had an influence on how the church changed as a whole.

The Vineyard Forte

To an evangelical outsider, the word that might best characterize the Vineyard movement's distinctiveness is "worship". Few issues have created so much angst, debate, and tension in churches—nearly always internally—than the subject of worship. What has always surprised me is how many of these heated conversations revolve around issues of form—hymns or choruses, organ or guitar, dancing or no dancing, and so on. However, few reformers have effectively reexamined the identity of this activity labeled with the cliché of "worship". Over the past quarter-century, a worship renewal has been sweeping western Christianity, and near its forefront has been the highly professional and intimately focused music spawned from local Vineyard churches around the world.[1] The Vineyard's founder and longtime leader, John Wimber, even named "contemporary worship in the freedom of the Holy Spirit" as one of the ten ingredients of the Vineyard Genetic Code. According to the Vineyard USA web site (2003), the primary reason Wimber's Calvary Chapel church joined a fledging group of Vineyard churches was worship-oriented: "As John and his congregation sought God in intimate worship they experienced empowerment by the Holy Spirit, significant renewal in the gifts and conversion growth. It became clear that the church's emphasis on the experience of the Holy Spirit was not shared by some leaders in the Calvary Chapel movement."

JV Understandings of Worship

It did not take long for me to recognize that worship held a special place in the life of JV. In many ways, it was completely typical for a Vineyard church: the singing of worship songs had a central place in their meetings, and music teams often played Vineyard-written songs, other contemporary worship tunes, or occasionally, an old hymn put to contemporary music. Another symptom of its cherished status was the high emphasis on quality; indeed, it would be difficult to ignore the fact that for a church of just over two hundred adults, four teams of completely different musicians all demonstrated impressively high musical

[1] For an outsider's perspective, see Percy (1997).

standards. From early on in the study, I noticed that worship was obviously a significant practice, and interaction with JVers overwhelmingly confirmed my suspicion. JVers loved to talk about the musical quality of their worship (over half pointed this out directly in the semi-structured interviews). One JVer described it as a "beautifully choreographed, sustained period of time with God" and one couple even said that "sometimes it's so good that we concentrate too much on the musicians." Worship was awarded such high merit based most significantly on this high standard of musical excellence, but also for the atmosphere which it created. Many JVers in their articulation of worship spoke of their individual preferences for having spiritual experiences, even those who were less externally expressive: "Personally, I don't tend to sing, but I love worship … I like to stand at the back and slide with the music. It's great time to just be still and concentrate on God." Ultimately, I concluded that JVers thought of worship as an opportunity for *an experiential, primarily emotional encounter with God aided by a pleasing musical style*.

Such sentiments, when added to the obvious Vineyard movement signature to JV's worship style, demonstrated to me that JV have definitely inherited Vineyard's music tradition. However, after a few months I began to see scattered traces that there was a subtle reluctance about this tradition. The most obvious hint was the scarcity of external expression during the times of singing. If one were to set up two cameras—one on the worship team leading the songs, and another on the JV congregation—I doubt that an outsider would associate them with each other. While a few JVers raised their hands above their heads and a handful more lifted them slightly, most JVers stood still while singing softly—if at all—while a decent number looked disinterested altogether. This, to me, was not characteristic of a Vineyard church, and I occasionally saw noticeable traces of frustration on the faces of the worship leaders, most likely spawned from a lack of reciprocated enthusiasm from the congregation. When I sought to test my observation with worship leaders themselves, I generally received confirmation of my suspicion, along with the additional sentiment, "We need to teach people how to worship, and that's a very tough thing to do." Thus on one hand, JVers would communicate repeatedly how much they prized and appreciated Sunday worship, yet on the other hand, their near-unresponsiveness during the actual act provoked and demanded further investigation.

Discontent and Experimentation

The second phase of my worship investigation pressed me past mere description; what I discovered was a sometimes voiced and sometimes yet-unrecognized discontent with the JV practice of worship. The first voices to express frustration to me were the participants in the worship teams themselves, all of whom manifested a considerable degree of reflection on the topic:

"We are definitely exploring the spirituality of our worship and it's in a metamorphosis sort of stage. I feel like there's another—or the next—paradigm of worship we haven't reached yet … I suggested to the worship band some time ago that just like Delirious and their Cutting Edge days, maybe that's where we are right now, in the nascent stages of spawning the next generation of worshippers … I'm also uneasy with the way in which worship songs sometimes don't follow the flow of a service or the talk: like yesterday, the final song killed the momentum of the service … Worship songs themselves are still a generation behind, especially the words … They need to get caught up with emerging church talks."

"Worship is much wider than singing songs, and [JV] need some teaching on this. We need a slight shift in understanding related to what worship is … At JV, there is no connection between Sunday morning worship and the God-connections made during the week; worship is too compartmentalized … The crisis is the bigger picture of merging what God is doing in your life with the Sunday morning thing so that it becomes a knitting together of behavior with belief: experience knitting into expression."

"Until recently, [the] Vineyard [movement] was considered to be the new and trendy thing … the music seems to be an indicator of a broader cultural issue … the Vineyard tradition of new instruments breaks the traditional associations people make with church. JV is pushing even these standards—for example, the use of strings—no arrangements are written for such things—but JV is laying the groundwork and challenging the idea that it's not about what we do. Vineyard is a very formulized way of doing church when it comes to church planting, worship, etc … But JV has questioned the formula, so nobody really knows where it's going.. We're trying to take a more holistic approach, experimenting with ideas for doing it. I used to do a pub service with [SWLV], but all we did was changed the style of the music—it was still a very modern way of worship. Now at JV, we've changed the style less and instead focused on the basic questions which underlie that, but we're nowhere near the answers to them."

"I went through a phase a few months ago where I was tired of the sameness of JV's worship, but now my spirits have been refreshed because I have a renewed desire to explore my relationship with Jesus through music … I think JV is in a good place right now because we're willing to explore and the desire is there to do so, though most [JVers] see experimentation as related to musical style. It's like trying to turn around an oil tanker with a very small rudder. Changing people's thinking takes time … In my eyes, [experimentation] should be mainly related to fresh lyrics which provoke a fresh experience in our relationship with God … It's figuring out how to write the same thing—'Jesus, I love you'—in a different way … It's almost like we've got to [as worship leaders] crawl out of the trenches, and we've been in so long and dug it so deep, that we've got to get out and see what else is going on."

I then took this idea of "transition" and tested it against the claims of JVers not involved in worship teams, asking them if JV were in a "worship transition". The response was thoroughly homogenous: "Definitely," one replied. "The boundaries are being pushed … There is a different sound, one which breaks out of the standard Vineyard sound … It's not the natural Vineyard thing. I think (names of two worship leaders) are really creative and are driving new ways of worship, but not everyone will like that." Another JVer added: "Yeah, I think so. You can see it in the way (worship leader's name) uses the keyboard and the different sounds there." Or, "God is putting some key people in place such as (names of three worship leaders). Their lives are called to the area of worship, and they're willing to challenge things." Though my question itself ("Is JV in a worship transition?") suggested no overtly musical slant, all respondents immediately began commenting on the musical aspect of JV's worship. In one conversation, the interviewee kept reiterating the line, "Things need to keep being different." I asked the JVer why. "So people don't get bored," he replied. "You have to be different things to different people." While a select few were able to discuss aspects of worship identity when prompted, the immediate association with the word "worship" was, in every case, linked to musical production. Whenever the quality of the worship came up as a topic, rarely did I run across any JVer speaking of a corporate experience of worship and even fewer communicated anything substantial about the underlying identity behind the practice of worship. One JVer who did manifest significant reflection on the topic said rather perceptively: "There is a huge chasm between what is portrayed and what the true nature of worship really is." While the more seasoned Christians would often insist on JV worship as being about more than singing songs and playing instruments, all the discussion of experimentation in worship revolved around the pragmatics of a musical presentation. Without putting it crassly, the metaphor which I have generated for worship at JV is "elevator music"—a means of creating a pleasant atmosphere, pointing to a sizable gap between the depth of experimentation they claimed to engender and what actually occurred. Interestingly, the one silent voice in the worship conversation is Lawton himself. Aside from the occasional reference, I had never heard him articulate, directly or indirectly, his own view on their congregational act of singing. According to the worship teams, he is almost entirely laissez-faire regarding what they do, and when I asked JVers to reflect upon what Lawton thinks about worship, they usually responded by saying "I don't really know."

To JV's credit, they have begun to experiment with ancient-future elements of faith (though the semi-structured interviews discovered that less than a sixth greatly appreciated these acts). Musical worship at JV is mostly characteristic of Webber's (2002) pragmatic evangelicals category: contemporary style, topical content, choruses, use of PowerPoint technology, presented by bands, and void of symbols (though towards the end of my fieldwork some video images were occasionally interjected during the singing). Webber contrasts these characteristics with the common attributes of younger evangelical worship (for example, liturgical/ancient-future style, Christian observance, strong use of symbols and icons, Scripture readings, participatory prayer), many of which coincide perfectly with the more recent ancient-future elements reoccurring in JV life with increasing frequency. JVers at all levels are unwilling to throw out either. The more Vineyard-minded JVers seemed to respect and appreciate the ancient-future elements of faith while those who enjoyed the latter still maintained high praise for the Vineyard-style worship. Even so, neither their pragmatic evangelical worship nor their liturgical elements were framed or refashioned in the context of their underlying identity transition towards discovering what it meant to be Christians in between the extremes of post-Christian culture and evangelicalism.

Incongruence and Contentment

As I was reflecting upon their worship practices, I began to notice that JV Sunday services seemed to be incongruous. It was not that the transition from the time of singing to the morning's talk was abrupt or disorderly, just that the two did not seem to be in harmony with one another. The incongruence extended beyond mere subject matter (for example, a set of worships songs with lyrics about grace, then a talk about the role of money): the philosophy behind Lawton's teaching was different from that of their practice of worship. One worship leader told me, "Our songs are really modern. Hopefully, as songwriters from the emerging church school of thought begin to write songs from a post-modern perspective, it will be reflected in the songs we sing." Yet I perceived that the incongruence issue at JV was not so much a question of style or content as it was of ethic. Though much of JV's teaching was spawned from, or at least evolving into, an "emerging church" school of thought (if such a thing can be said to exist), their practice of worship was still thoroughly Vineyard; while experimentation with different sounds and interludes of Scripture readings and/or prayers may have been occurring on an occasional basis, even that genre of experimentation itself is very characteristic of the Vineyard movement and EPC churches in general.

One final illustration may demonstrate this metamorphosis well. One of the JV worship team leaders was asked to give a Sunday talk about worship; this JVer seemed to have two distinct and very different halves to his talk (though it did not strike me as careless or inauthentic at all). He began by citing ample biblical evidence that "worship" is about far more than singing, stressing that it is about our everyday lives; Sunday singing, in his words, is "a continuation of our worship to God throughout the week." He then, in the very different latter half of his talk, made little mention of these ideas or connection to them, exclusively focusing on their current musical style. He argued for musical style as "something people need to be flexible with" because it is a means of evangelism both to their kids and their non-Christian friends. At first, I myself responded to the talk rather negatively in my own mind, but upon further reflection and conversations with a handful of JVers, I came to realize that it demonstrated well the duality of their incongruence issue. On one hand, they have grown fond of the Vineyard worship tradition (whether it is their own musical preference or just habituation to the norms of a Sunday service), but on the other hand, their evolving identity necessitates a revisitation of the underlying identity of worship. So while synergy may elude them (as it appeared so in this JVer's discourse), awkward coexistence is the best option in the meantime.

Dual Approaches

During one conversation with Lawton, I asked if he himself noticed this incongruence. "Oh yes," he replied. "It sticks out a mile to me. But we went through a phase of throwing everything out, and decided that some stuff was worth keeping." While I believe a carefulness to be non-reactionary is beneficial, I wondered why their practice of worship has not undergone the process of rethinking Lawton claims when he says that "if you scratch below the surface [of our] programs, you might find some philosophical and theological assumptions that are different." To summarize, I suggest that JV worship represents their tension between a pragmatic-evangelical mindset and its forms encountering what might be labeled a "post-pragmatic" identity which concerns itself with intangible values such as maturity and mystery. Put differently, there was a tension between a "code of doing" and a "mode of being". When JVers on any level sensed a discomfort in worship (that is, a lack of "relevance"), their automatic response was a reformulation of pragmatics—musical quality, arrangement of instruments, generation of new sounds or songs, and so on. However, Lawton's sermons, whilst they once were extremely typical of pragmatic evangelicalism (according to longtime JVers), were increasingly moving away from the "code of doing" paradigm to a "mode of being" paradigm. However, the pragmatic, "code of doing" mindset still has primary influence on JV's worship "transition", and until JV generate an ethic by which to reconstruct their worship on a basis of renewed identity (pertaining to who they are and what worship is) instead of changing aesthetics, their transition may be incomplete and counterproductive. While rethinking their identity may very well involve refashioned aesthetics as one necessary implication, I still wondered if JV could effectively teach Christians to rethink what it meant to be Christian and be a church while their most widely shared congregational practice weekly reemphasizes the values of revising aesthetics according to personal taste.

The Reconstruction Crisis

Worship at JV thus points to the larger concept of reconstruction. Though I will utilize the phrase "reconstruction crisis", never did I sense they were in a state of imminent crisis, but rather a dilemma of a more subtle—though equally as thorough—genre. Most JVers have found themselves in a communal struggle (sometimes against and sometimes alongside each other) to discover their individual identity as Christians and members of their culture and how to authentically construct a community as very different people in a very different setting without becoming entirely disconnected from themselves, each other, and their backgrounds. Essentially, JV seemed to be trapped (for lack of a better word) between the necessity of change (both internal and external) and the fear of losing that which makes them who they are. Naturally, questions such as: "What does make us who we are?", "Can we change what we do and still be who we are?", and "What do we reject and what do we keep?" are implicit in such a context. When a JV practice did not "make sense" or seem "relevant" to congregants, it caused a certain level of discomfort (whether recognizable or not) between those more willing to reform or reject traditions and those who preferred to keep or redefine them.

Put differently, JVers are struggling to fill the void left by those things which they have deconstructed. It might be illustrated by this formula:

> "If not [practice or belief], then what? And why—on what basis?"

To illustrate, the "messy spirituality" series raised the question, "If not spirituality as conformity, then what? And why—on what basis?" While the "then what?" question may be more tangibly felt, the "on what basis?" query is even more significant, pointing to a desire for something to legitimate their choices about spirituality. In a similar way, the logic of evangelism led to the same question. I have already noted the unanimous rejection of hard-sell evangelism amongst JVers. But I also found it a common sentiment that no one was entirely sure how to handle issues of faith with the unchurched. "If not hard-sell evangelism, then what? And on what basis?" According to Jamieson (2002, p. 163), many in liminal groups such as JV "have through personal experience come to the point that Paul Ricoeur (1967) talked of as 'beyond the desert of criticism, where we wished to be called again'. That is, the place that seeks to reconstruct a faith out of the pieces of the past and the new understandings drawn from the personal journey into exile." One JVer concurred with his wife's comments about the presence of gray faith at JV (as opposed to viewing truth through a black and white, absolutist lens) by noting that "the more liberal view also creates questions. How do I relate to other religions now? Or gays? It's good that I can be accepting and nonjudgmental, but on a mental-theological note, I'm not sure where I stand now." He directly followed this sentiment by saying, "But I'm OK with that because that's part of maturity." One JV couple, in response to my question about JV's identity in relation to other churches, replied by saying that JV are a "melting pot" because they are attempting to "reinvent themselves, using elements of everything, and figuring out how to bring all those elements into a cohesive whole, even though some things sometimes seem conflicting …." These issues were part of this larger struggle I have labeled the "reconstruction crisis", a situation implicitly calling for some sort of criteria or ethic of discernment by which to make such decisions.

For JV, the task is not the adoption of an already established set of values or norms, but rather the creation of a new identity and lens of interpretation altogether, one which will enable them as a community to filter out certain practices, reform/

redefine others, and fuse new ones into their life. I therefore identified this as JV's central theological question: What are our criteria for reconstruction which result in relevance to ourselves and those to whom we are trying to credibly represent the Christian faith?

Chapter 5

Reflections for a Wider Context

Generalization in Qualitative Research

As demonstrated in Chapter 1, the practical theological process involves a church analyzing its own situation and reflecting theologically upon it in an effort to generate more effective and faithful practices. Using the tools of qualitative research, a community of faith can do this via a congregational study. Surely a congregational study has relevance for its own participants, but what, if any, meaning can emerge for practitioners in other settings? Should a congregational study yield universal norms? Must it yield norms at all, even for the researched group? Some within the field of contemporary practical theology, as explained in Chapter 1, argue that it ought to work to paint a normative vision of the human life cycle; however, I concur with those who believe that practical theology is transformational by offering new questions and training communities of faith to better participate in "the mission of God". As this congregational study moves beyond the local JV situation to consider its ramifications for other settings, it must ask the question of what kinds of findings will emerge when social science methods are used so integrally in the practical theological process? To what extent will they be applicable to other contexts? Will they be commensurable with practical theology?

The field of qualitative research continues to undergo its own debates as to what kinds of findings it is capable of producing. Fortunately, what is emerging from those discussions is similar to the genre of insights practical theology is capable of producing, and looking briefly at some of these authors will clarify the types of insights a congregational study will produce, since it is a marriage of practical theology and ethnography.

Sociological theory is moving beyond a polarity between positivism (a tradition which seeks universal truths because all societies, like nature, operate according to discernible laws) and naturalism (a tradition which produces rich accounts of situations without emphasizing their applicability to other settings). While there is no definite model for relating ideas and empirical data in the social sciences, I will draw upon three of the main influences in the field addressing this tension in constructing a mode of developing theoretical generalizations which practical theology can orient toward its own cause.

Herbert Blumer (1969) was one of the first to offer an alternative with the notion of "sensitizing concepts". For him, sensitizing concepts refer to ideas that merely provide directions along which to look rather than provide descriptions of what to see. They are interpretive devices whose value lies in guiding empirical research rather than satisfying the requirements of epistemological purists. Sensitizing concepts are not fixed, but can be refined and developed through viewing them from different angles, asking many different questions of them, and returning to more scrutiny from the standpoint of such questions.

With similar motivations, Barney Glaser and Anselm Strauss (1967) developed grounded theory.[1] Glaser and Strauss propose that social research and generating theory should go hand in hand, that data collection and analysis should occur simultaneously. It also puts emphasis on developing new theories, not testing preexisting ones. Put simply, grounded theory is rooted in empirical data, and moves to more general theory by an ongoing process of comparing concept with data, and concept with concept. For these reasons, Glaser and Strauss also describe grounded theory as the "constant comparative method". The type of theory which Glaser and Strauss (and many of their followers) have sought to produce is not "grand theory" as the positivists desire, nor minor theories applicable only to the specific setting being studied. Instead, they are sociological ideas and concepts capable of interacting with other sociological ideas and concepts. By this, Glaser and Strauss mean that grounded theoretical concepts will yield a "meaningful" picture enabling one to grasp what is being portrayed in terms of one's own experience. While grounded theory is now associated with a wide range of specific methods of collecting and coding data, it began simply as a way of having ideas based on empirical data.[2]

Though grounded theory has expanded to connote a wide and very structured variety of data collection and analytic techniques, I chose not to identify the JV congregational study explicitly with grounded theory. However, the ethos of grounded theory did help me to move from observational data to the themes in Chapter 3, and now to the reflections contained later in this chapter. Grounded theorists collect and then immediately code their data (whether they be from observations, conversations, interviews, reflections, or documents) in order to define and categorize it. From these categories, central themes are selected and a storyline about the people, social process, or situation is constructed consistent with these classifications. These themes can then be compared with those of other contexts.

A third voice upon which many social researchers have also drawn is Charles Peirce's (1979) philosophical work on abductive reasoning.[3] Peirce used abductive reasoning and logic to contrast with the polar opposites of inductive and deductive logic. Inductivism is based on the assumption that laws or generalizations can be generated by accumulating observations and cases and noticing regularities over time. Deductive reasoning maintains that empirical research can only be used to test theories, thus confining inquiry to the realm of testing existing

[1] For reviews, see Charmaz (2000) and Strauss and Corbin (1990).

[2] For a discussion of how grounded theory has become more identified with practical procedures than processes of thinking, see Atkinson, Coffey, and Delamont, (2003, pp. 148–52).

[3] For a brief review, see Kelle (1998).

ideas and limiting the development of new theories. Peirce's approach sought to capture more effectively the way researchers in all fields actually think and study, advocating a strong role for empirical research while maintaining a dynamic play between the data and ideas. In abductive reasoning, the researcher starts from the local, identifying a particular or surprising phenomenon, and then connecting it with other, broader concepts. This is done in comparative fashion by inspecting one's personal experience, one's stock of knowledge of similar phenomena, and the equivalent stock of ideas and frameworks gleaned from within one's discipline and those neighboring it. Abductive reasoning does not settle for categorizing the data into existing ideas, nor does it merely seek to undermine existing theories. The data are used to generate new configurations of ideas, new possibilities, and imaginative ways of thinking about what is being researched.

There is not one, "correct" interpretation of a social setting, nor is there a universally accepted protocol for theorizing in the social sciences. The ideas of Blumer, Glaser and Strauss, and Peirce have elaborated upon a common way of thinking about the purpose of qualitative research, a way of using empirical data and theoretical ideas which many researchers have employed in various ways and with different emphases. While loyalty to sound heuristic principles must be retained, allegiance to a strict model of analysis and generalization is not necessary. They can be utilized and adapted in a variety of ways without losing their force or sacrificing logical integrity. In summarizing this way of thinking, Amanda Coffey and Paul Atkinson (1996, p. 162) note that:

> [w]hen we study local manifestations of culture and social order, we do not have to assume that such social worlds are representative of wider populations … On the other hand, our ideas are not confined to the detailed description of the local. In developing and refining, or indeed creating, concepts we aim … to transcend the local and the particular. Abductive inferences lead us from specific cases or findings toward generic levels that allow us to move conceptually across a wide variety of social contexts.

In the same way, practical theology looks for ways to make its insights useful for other contexts and ones which ultimately enable transformation. Consequently, the sort of practical theological reflection which this inquiry will pursue is the explication from empirical research of comparative concepts which can travel across a variety of ecclesial contexts to guide further inquiry and provide potential points of practical theological reflection which may enable responses of critical faithfulness.

Drawing from the themes which emerged from the fieldwork, I have identified five such comparable concepts. The treatment of each will seek to:

- illustrate how the concept arose from the empirical findings of the JV congregational study;

- demonstrate why reflection on the concept (and its role in the life of Jacobsfield Vineyard) may be transformational for other church contexts, with specific attention given to the "emerging church";
- suggest specific, related lines of further inquiry and exploration for churches and theological disciplines such as historical theology, systematic theology, or biblical theology.

I will first look specifically at these five comparable concepts which the JV congregational study raises for other churches. Then I will conclude by offering recommendations for the field of practical theology spawned from this congregational study.

Comparable Concepts Raised by the Congregational Study

Since JV's central question of "What are our criteria for reconstruction which result in relevance to ourselves and those to whom we are trying to credibly represent the Christian faith?" arose from the empirical findings of the study, bringing together the themes I identified in Chapter 3 which comprise their identity, it can serve as a helpful blueprint for giving attention to the issues which this congregational study has raised. In this section, I will consider a concept related to each of the four aspects of JV's identity—relating to religious parentage, safe places, Christian growth and maturity, and communication with contemporary culture—as well as a fifth regarding the challenges of reconstruction.

Relating to Religious Parentage

The first comparative concept is the difficult and complex challenge of relating to religious parentage. Chapter 3 demonstrated that JVers viewed evangelicalism as a point of reference and departure. They stubbornly maintained an identity of "different-ness" in spite of their reluctance at being entirely disconnected from their religious roots. Consequently, they were engaged in a habit of sifting through the contents of the evangelical faith which they were given, concluding that some aspects (most notably conversion strategies) could be discarded while others must be retained. For some JVers, this process concerned aesthetics such as creatively using instruments during worship times or utilizing audio-visual technology in the Sunday services. For others, it demanded a reconsideration of sexual ethics, authority structures, or the nature of the Christian message.

The JV congregational study thus serves to alert other churches to the difficult task of appropriating their faith traditions in a rapidly changing cultural climate. It encourages them to intentionally wrestle with this challenge and to do so in a critical, constructive, and credible manner. Churches can heighten their awareness of the ways in which their specific religious tradition has shaped them and—if they are negatively reacting to it—the ways in which it continues to influence that process. Moreover, one's parental faith must be seen as interwoven with broader cultural influences. Religious traditions—both the propositional contents of belief and the habits or rituals by which belief is expressed—do not form and take shape in a culture-neutral way; they influence and are influenced by the surrounding cultural climate. Their stories are distinguishable, yet closely interconnected. In JV's case, their frustration with evangelicalism, it could be said, arose in part as a result of members operating within a cultural situation increasingly different than the one in which evangelicalism took shape. Webber (2002) argues that conservative Christianity (evangelicals and the Vineyard movement included) has sought to operate within a very scientific, modern worldview. Since many (though not all) JVers have been raised in a more pluralistic context, they were more likely to resist definitive claims of how church should be done or how Christians must behave. For other churches, acknowledging the contingency of their expressions and beliefs upon historical shifts and reactionary responses to other traditions may engender a more humble and critical adoption and adaptation of their tradition.

A scene from JV may further assist in illustrating the difficulty of this task. As I mentioned in Chapter 3, one of Lawton's primary three questions at JV was "What does it mean to be a Christian?" This also manifested itself consistently with church members, albeit with a narrower spectrum of concern. At the October 2003 meeting of Journey, their version of a theological roundtable, Lawton was attempting to focus the discussion on reading the Bible through what he termed a "nonfoundationalist lens of interpretation". He explained that modernism viewed knowledge as bricks stacked one on top of another; post-modernism, on the other hand, viewed it as a web, and he illustrated by placing a can of snack food in the middle of the circle, noting how everyone would describe it slightly differently from their various viewpoints. Despite his efforts to focus the conversation on this epistemological difference, ultimately the topic which drew a majority of attendees' interest (as it did in previous meetings of Journey) was clarifying the criteria for being a Christian as a means to get into heaven and avoid hell. The question which catalyzed the prolonged discussion (posed by a JVer at the meeting) was, "Well, how do [Lawton's comments on biblical interpretation] affect John 14:6 where Jesus said 'I am the way, the truth, and the life. No man comes to the Father except through me'?" For JVers, the immediate implication for altering one's view on Christian truth directly related to the entrance requirements for entering heaven. Essentially, "being a Christian" for many JVers was something to be obtained, maintained, and then enjoyed when one enters the afterlife. This sentiment, confirmed by findings elsewhere, stands in contrast to the fact that not once in the fieldwork period did Lawton or any JVer present in a Sunday meeting an invitation to Christianity on the basis of an afterlife in heaven. Since such a large number of JVers passionately guarded this view of the Christian life, it could be said that even if commonly held assumptions are not regularly articulated publicly, they are still likely to be existent and internally operative. JVers seemed unable or unwilling to call such a central interpretation into question, pointing to the challenging duty of critiquing one's religious parentage without being severed from it.

In Chapter 1, Farley (1983) and Fowler (1999) demonstrated that contemporary practical theology encourages churches to mirror biblical writers and figures throughout Christian history who responded creatively to the needs of their situations while remaining faithful to the divine reality which had apprehended them. The objective, they argue, is not to methodically apply their solutions, but to imitate their diligence in carefully and inventively addressing the current needs of churches as they attempt to embody the mission of God in the world today. Theological reflection, therefore, must be able to provide embodied Christian responses to complex situations while at the same time challenging a church's current understandings of what makes it Christian. Reflecting theologically on religious parentage will pose new questions to other theological disciplines. It will ask historical theology to provide accounts of the evolution of various religious traditions with ample detail about and analysis of their relationships to their respective socio-cultural contexts,[4] particularly in light of the current challenges of pluralism. By illustrating the interdependence of theological systems and ideas on cultural factors, historical theology can encourage Christians to be more humble about and open to rethinking their ideas of what it means to be Christian.

Yet this awareness, even of a historical theological genre, is not enough to enable transformation. Intentional engagement with ecclesiology, the doctrine of the Church, will bolster the integrity of churches in being faithful both to their religious parents and the demands of their situation in a number of ways. First, for churches in the process of sifting and discerning their tradition in deciding what to retain, what to alter, and what to leave behind, an informed ecclesiology will prevent them from making these choices based solely on aesthetic preference or personal tastes. Second, it will address any fears of changes resulting in being "cut off" from Christianity or disloyal to it. Third, it will reinforce and stress the communal dimensions of the Christian faith, namely how the congregation as a corporate body may function as a mediation of Christ to the world; this is a particularly timely emphasis for an increasingly individualistic[5] and consumerist western culture.[6] Finally, it will remind churches of their participatory role in the mission of God and enable churches to appreciate and assess how their religious parents may or may not have been participating in the mission of God in their own contexts, settings which have varying degrees of (dis)similarity to their own.

While all churches may benefit from considering this comparative concept, it is especially pertinent for those which identify themselves with the emerging church. Chapter 3 linked JV to what Jamieson (2002) calls "liminal churches"; the concept of liminality may also be a very helpful way of looking at the emerging church. Though this concept has found its way into the discussions of many academic

[4] See Schreiter's (1985) work regarding the inseparable relationship between tradition, theology, and culture.

[5] For academic discussions of individualism, see Bellah *et al.* (1985) and Triandis (1995).

[6] For an academic discussion of consumerism, see Campbell (1987).

disciplines, it can be traced to Arnold van Gennep's (1960) research on rites of passage which was later pursued and popularized by the work of Victor Turner (1969, 1974, 1982). Gennep's theory advocated three stages to a rite of passage: pre-liminal, liminal, and post-liminal. Liminality in Turner's thought referred to the second stage in any status-changing ritual. The first stage, what he labels separation, invoked a leaving of a certain status or affiliation. Before the person's new status is confirmed (the third, post-liminal stage of reincorporation), there is a second stage, the liminal phase; this is the one to which he gives the greatest attention. Liminality, he explains, comes from the Latin word *līmen* which means "a threshold". It is characterized by ambiguity, openness, and indeterminacy. One's sense of identity dissolves to some extent, bringing about disorientation because the individual is "betwixt and between", neither one thing or another. It is a transitional period during which one relaxes one's usual limits to thought, self-understanding, and behavior, thus opening the way to something new.

The most obvious examples of liminality are the ethnographic studies of traditional peoples initiating adolescent boys into manhood. While details and complexity vary greatly, the underlying trend in these rituals is the same. The boys are forcefully taken from their families and villages to a remote place where they are subjected to various trials or humiliations by older men. This may last anywhere from a few days to a few months, occasionally even years. At the end, they are returned to the village in a strongly ritualistic reunion; often the boys are considered to have died and been reborn as men. They may be given new names and "taught" to recognize their friends and relatives. In essence, there is an extended stage in which the individual is no longer a boy but not yet a man, a "betwixt and between" state. As a result, this phase of liminality is both individual and collective. In fact, he gives great attention to the kind of relations which emerge between those undergoing liminality, something which he calls "communitas" in which participants experience an enormous amount of intimacy and equality with one another.[7]

Viewing the emerging church movement as a liminal group raises many good questions and points of reflection. Turner (1974) uses the analogy of a pilgrimage (also implying, of course, that a literal pilgrimage is a liminal experience), a potentially illuminating concept in light of the emerging church's self-proclaimed purposes. These practitioners have decisively moved on from something—in most cases, conservative evangelicalism—but have not yet arrived at another definite mode of being. Similarly, those on a pilgrimage, Turner notes, expect to arrive at a place where they will directly experience something sacred, whether miraculous healing or inward transformation. Their "emerging church" label itself attempts to imply the indefiniteness and transitory nature of their development. While Turner is quick to note the opportunistic promise of liminal groups, he and other writers

[7] For a detailed account, see Turner (1969). For critiques, see Eade and Sallnow (1991) and Dutton (2008). For related discussions of liminality, see the contributions in Brown (2002).

on liminality do not hesitate to note that the phase has its own set of challenges. The directional fragility and developmental confusion manifested at Jacobsfield Vineyard may sensitize other emerging church practitioners to the dangers of liminality on the shadow side of its necessities and opportunities.

In light of the challenges of liminality, one primary need for emerging churches may be the task of making explicit their theological and religious beliefs and suppositions, and then to critically appraise them. If they want to retain a Christian identity while being distinguished from evangelicalism, what exactly does this entail? Is the process of differentiation an ambiguous one based on personal preferences? Is it the adoption of new sets of beliefs, or a different genre of belief altogether? What role does the Bible and Christian tradition play? Put simply, this journey cannot take place in a theological vacuum. Fortunately, there are ample resources to consult.[8] For example, by gleaning from the disciplines of systematic and biblical theology, emerging churches may gain a better sense of the central themes of the mission of God, and of the ways in which the Church is obligated to be continually reformed and redirected to the needs of the world. Historical theology may create an awareness of how theological understandings evolve and why their religious parents held to certain claims of truth. Consulting these disciplines will help churches to decipher what inherited theological perspectives to retain and which to modify or discard, and save them from the trap of reconstruction according to personal tastes, disconnected from the Christian tradition. Lawton spoke of JV responding theologically as opposed to reacting sociologically, as he claimed some emerging church groups tended to do. JVers were asking pertinent theological questions and Lawton was undoubtedly engaged in much theological reflection himself. Consequently, JV were certainly not reconstructing their identity in a theological vacuum, though they demonstrated little consensus about the process itself.

Moreover, JV's story may enlighten emerging churches as to aspects in which they are not different than their religious parents, wrestling with the same theological and relational issues as the groups from which they departed. Considering to what extent the emerging church is a liminal movement may draw intriguing comparisons to transitional times in church history (or even liminal groups in secular history and society). Is the emerging church typical, the natural result of a changing cultural context and the outworking of difficulties within evangelicalism and its interpretations of Christianity? For instance, does it resemble groups in the Protestant Reformation or John Wesley's Methodism,[9] groups who were discontent with their religious parents' theological understandings and their inability or unwillingness to meet the needs of their cultural setting? While it

[8] Some emerging church writers have noticed the lack of focused theological reflection among emerging churches and produced works to address the issue. See McLaren (2003) and Grenz and Franke (2001).

[9] For an overview of these movements and more, see Gonzales (1985), Kolb (1991), and Cracknell and White (2005).

would be pretentious to see the emerging church as a microcosm of the Church of the future, it may be credible to suggest that they provide pointers to aspects in which the Church will be overhauled in the years to come, sensitizing churches to significant areas of reflection.

Despite the post- or anti-evangelical posture of emerging churches, dialogue with EPC congregations may be one of the wisest decisions for emerging churches wishing to effectively relate to their religious parents. If one follows Webber's designations of traditional evangelicals, pragmatic evangelicals, and younger evangelicals (2002), emerging churches may realize that they too, much like their pragmatic parents, are attempting to be relevant in ways they perceive their parents as being irrelevant. This common basis of reformation and relevance may not only help each group to come to appreciative understandings of one another, but inspire cooperation in initiatives where they both see the mission of God at work.

Furthermore, for churches which may fall into Webber's categories of traditional or pragmatic evangelicals (or Jamieson's EPC classification), encountering the story of an emerging church may help them to discover more about themselves. Lawton found solidarity in the emerging church conversation because others there were struggling with their relationship to evangelicalism, and when he began to openly challenge its norms, others in the JV congregation resonated with his sentiments, and many newcomers were also attracted. For other evangelical practitioners, Lawton's story and other similar ones may provoke a journey of self-evaluation of which two opposite dangers exist. The first is assuming that they themselves have nothing to offer, or are outdated entirely. Evangelicalism has strengths and contributions which they must maintain, advantages from which emerging churches in their journeys of differentiation may still benefit. On the opposite extreme, they may also neglect to bring their own praxis under scrutiny, assuming that the discontent of the younger evangelicals and their churches is symptomatic of immaturity or a compromise of Christian mission. An attitude of critical listening to the complaints and insights of their offspring may be a helpful catalyst for transformation in their own ranks.

Safe Places

A second comparative concept meriting reflection is the notion of safe places. The JV congregational study revealed a central significance to the church's climate of safety. In fact, when probed about the distinctiveness of their church, JVers most often replied with descriptions pointing to JV as a safe place to be themselves, share weaknesses, or voice doubts. In short, to use their favored term, JV was a place where they could "be real". They consistently claimed Lawton's transparent leadership and an accepting network of relationships to be responsible for this. This concept of safe places may provoke useful reflection in other churches on how and why such safe places may be created and when, I will suggest, it might be appropriate to create unsafe places.

This congregational study may encourage churches to first honestly examine their own relational atmospheres. Why have congregants joined, why do they stay, and why do some leave? Since many JVers left previous churches and joined JV for relational reasons related to acceptance of their weaknesses and space to "be real", this may cause churches to investigate whether or not a similar atmosphere characterizes their own church. They may do this by way of an informal survey or via casual interviews, but it is important to explore questions related to why members remain, how many relationships they have formed at the church, and how they might characterize the depth of those connections. Practically, this may be a challenging task, particularly if congregants do not feel safe to be critically open about their church. As churches enter into this process of situational analysis, they will be better poised to engage in the even more difficult activity of implementing change in the "safety" of their relational atmospheres.

JVers' emphasis on Lawton's role in creating this atmosphere may prompt senior church leaders to consider their own role in cultivating transparency. It can be assumed that without Lawton's transparent leadership—for example, his repeated affirmations of his own weaknesses, frustrations, lack of confidence, or uncertainty about some aspects of Christianity—JV would not have developed a similar outlook. Many JVers spoke of a "permission-giving" impact his leadership style had on people coming to a greater acceptance of their own weaknesses and those of others. This is not to pose Lawton's leadership style as an ideal type, but simply to challenge church leaders to come to greater awareness of their own character's extrapolated influence upon the relational atmosphere of their churches. It may also cause them to reflect upon and rethink their own notion of what it means for them to lead and steward their faith communities. What is the relationship between a leader and their people? In what ways can a minister effectively and appropriately use transparency in leading a congregation? What is the best time and place for transparency?

Another potential strategy for creating safe places is a greater teaching emphasis on the theological concept of community.[10] Churches cannot be left to their own cultural preferences when formulating models of community. Sustained and repeated attention on Jesus' vision for love within the Church, such as the passage in John 17, may be a helpful starting point. This teaching emphasis may also highlight the early church as recorded in the book of Acts, with special attention given to the dilemmas of inclusion and exclusion which first-century Christians faced. Further on in the New Testament, it could potentially track Paul's usage of the concept of *koinonia*. Looking to post-biblical Christian history, churches could explore the ways in which historical Christians created or failed to create safe places. Whatever the spectrum of theological resources employed, it is essential to stress that shaping relational atmospheres is not merely a social task, but a deeply theological one as well. This will prompt exploration in the theological disciplines

[10] Though their critics are many, the theological concept of community is explored in Hauerwas and Willimon (1989). See also Hauerwas (1981).

of systematic and historical theology, particularly by bringing questions related to acceptance, inclusion, and forgiveness in a pluralistic and fragmented world to their studies.

One area in which JV's life may be strategically illuminating is in the relationship between permitting doubts about the Christian faith and interpersonal acceptance. As the semi-structured interviews showed, only a minority of JVers had undergone significant crises of faith in which they struggled ideologically with Christianity, though that was a crucial turning point in Lawton's story. While JVers defended anyone's right to question the Christian faith or remain undecided about it while participating in the life of their church, there was not much explicit "doubting" visibly taking place. JVers themselves did not indicate a great need to deconstruct Christianity, but their priority on accepting people automatically entailed an acceptance of ideological uncertainty. If one connects this motif with the larger state of ideological pluralism and the aversion to metanarratival truth symptomatic of western culture, one could say that JV's attitude is naturally quite appealing for the current cultural setting, perhaps accounting for the relatively large number of adherents with a more ideologically flexible worldview.

In a post-industrial world where ideas and worldviews not only become consumer goods to be adopted, mixed, and discarded as one chooses, but also serve as signifiers of individual identity, ideological freedom is at a high premium. Since human thoughts are one of the most central things which constitute individuality, respecting one's ability to think differently is one of the deepest expressions of holistic acceptance. Churches which meaningfully listen and those who tolerate, build upon, and give safe space for ideological discussion—even of the beliefs historically most central to the Christian faith—are likely to gain a greater audience in and develop a closer relationship with contemporary culture than those who do not. In this way, the emerging church's liminality may be a great advantage. While liminality can produce anxiety in some, for many people today indeterminateness in spiritual and religious matters may be very attractive.

However, the comparative concept of safe space may also be seen in a different light. "Safe space" ought not to be regarded as a desirable characteristic of a church at all times. Practical theological reflection also necessitates consideration of to what extent a climate of safety is not appropriate for the Christian faith. For instance, in what ways do the resources of the Christian faith demand that churches be uncomfortable and risky places? How does the Christian story challenge existing views and habits? While a safe place for ideological uncertainty is apparently effective in making room for people with a less dogmatic attitude, is there a danger of ideological apathy? Chapter 1 demonstrated that contemporary practical theology emphasizes the necessary role of transformation. Theological reflection in the practical theological process is meant, on the one hand, to question existing interpretations of Christianity, but also, on the other hand, to confront churches with the Christian faith in an encounter which transforms them into an embodied response to the needs of their situation.

A beneficial starting point in wrestling with these questions may be the biblical theme of prophecy.[11] In the Jewish history, a prophet's purpose was often to courageously call a nation or people group to account for their treatment of the poor and disadvantaged, their affinity with other gods, or another shortcoming in the sight of God. Prophets were meant to make the lives of their hearers uncomfortable for the sake of faithful change. The prophetic ministry of Jesus continues this theme in the New Testament; he often directed spoken and embodied criticisms against the religious communities of his day, judging their notions of what it meant to be honorable in God's eyes as inadequate and even corrupt. Furthermore, the New Testament attests to a prophetic ministry for the Church as commissioned by Jesus. For church leaders to be faithful to the theological theme of prophecy, there will inevitably be times when they are forced to create uncomfortable and "unsafe" spaces for their people. However, this will be a very careful and delicate task.

The movement of situational analysis in the practical theological process will be an essential ingredient in fulfilling this prophetic function because it can identify aspects of culture which need to be creatively addressed by the Christian tradition. At Jacobsfield Vineyard, Lawton sometimes spoke of Christianity as "an alternative basis for living", a choice to live according to a different set of values and criteria for success than the surrounding world. While JVers readily explained (when asked) what Lawton meant by this phrase, it never surfaced in their understandings of Christian life and ministry. Other churches may ask themselves how they can be prophetic. For instance, how might churches become communities which provide an alternative to the aspects of consumerism which are incommensurable with Christian mission? To even reach the point of embodying such an alternative, the congregation itself must be prophetically challenged and confronted with the mission of God and their own tendencies as consumers. Therefore, while churches may benefit from becoming places of holistic acceptance, there is also the obligation of transformation.

As a result, the need to create socially-appropriate and theologically-faithful unsafe places will also ask a few things of theological disciplines. For biblical theology, it will ask for vivid descriptions of the early church's inclusion and exclusion dilemmas, described in such a way that contemporary Christians will be able to see their own parallel situations more clearly. Biblical and systematic theology will also be requested to provide not only explication of prophetic texts, but a robust array of resources and metaphors related to the role of prophecy in the faith community, both on individual and corporate levels and leadership and lay levels. For christology, it will request a rich picture of Jesus as a prophet amidst ideologies and values contrary to the kingdom of God, and the ways in which he commissioned the Church to continue this function.[12]

---

[11] For a discussion of prophecy, see Brueggemann (1978).

[12] Some starting points may be Wright (2000), Yoder (1994), and Wink (1984).

Of particular importance to emerging churches will be the question of how safe to make their spaces for post-evangelical Christians. At JV, Lawton's crisis early in the church's history paved the way for an influx of discontented evangelicals. In a parallel manner, the emerging church is the byproduct of evangelicals breaking ranks and forming new churches. Emerging churches would do well to scrutinize this, their greatest strength and reason for existence, for ways in which it may also be a weakness. On the one hand, emerging churches have demonstrated a special attractiveness to people (Christian or not) skeptical of religious institutions, and this forte should not be undervalued or underutilized. On the other hand, creating spaces to heal and restore confidence in Christianity must not come at the expense of the obligation of the Christian message. In other words, in becoming something other than certain expressions of being Christian, emerging churches must be careful to not become something less than Christian. This then relates directly to the next theme emerging from the study.

Christian Growth and Maturity

A third comparable concept which may prompt useful reflection is Christian growth and maturity. The JV congregational study revealed that while there was an implicit expectation for maturity at Jacobsfield Vineyard, there was also a very individual orientation to it, a wide diversity of definition concerning it, and no consensus on the resources for achieving it. It was a largely unresolved issue which was seldom (if ever) addressed directly, but desperately needed attention. It is very likely that other churches share to some degree a similar quandary of defining Christian maturity and identifying strategies for cultivating it, especially in an era of increased pluralism and difference.

The concept of Christian development naturally leads to the function and discipline of Christian education. Whether or not "Christian education" is an official program or a frequently used phrase in a church, within a congregation the dynamics of growth and maturity are at work, whether they are explicit, implicit, or a mixture of both. As a result, an initial step for churches may be an investigative look at their existing criteria for Christian growth and maturity. What do congregants view as the characteristics of a mature individual? Where do these characteristics originate and how do they correlate with the Christian tradition? How much or how little consensus is there within the church about who Christians are to become? Do congregants view the church as a whole as being on a journey of maturity? And if so, where along that journey are they? Exploring questions (in, perhaps, a similar way to those mentioned in the previous section) such as these will most likely discredit some existing assumptions about what is or is not valued amongst members and provide a useful starting point.

To use the example of JV, their enthusiastic embrace of the "messy spirituality" series demonstrated that there was a strong sense of relief over the lack of formulas and rules for fashioning one's spirituality, but this relief was not mirrored by a matching enthusiasm for replacing these formulas with resources for constructing Christian growth and maturity. The semi-structured interviews confirmed that JVers had a wide and sometimes ambiguous spectrum for judging or communicating spiritual maturity. It is possible that churches who share a parallel stance of deconstruction and disaffection with evangelicalism may also reflect similar sentiments to those expressed by JVers. Yet practical theological reflection must interrogate such an approach to spirituality. As suggested in the previous section, critical faithfulness necessitates the creation of safe places to "be real" where the "messiness" of human existence is accepted and embraced. However, it also demands transformation and unsafe places where people are challenged to mature. Consequently, the JV congregational study also prompts reflection on how practical theology may facilitate a move beyond "messy spirituality". To be sure, JV identified this need, but seemed uncertain as to how to move on in some decisive way.

The comparative encounter for other church contexts comes in considering the more developed dimensions of the Christian life and how Christian education might avoid developmental apathy by providing resources for growth. Since practical theology is an unending cycle, churches may be encouraged to conceive of spirituality as a journey, taken with others, which demands continual growth and adaptation to a variety of challenges. Embracing the starting point of spiritual journeyers is a valuable emphasis of a messy spirituality approach, but churches may also do these explorers the favor of creating a climate of developmental expectation. Jamieson (2002) catalogues the journeys of leavers outside of church, but the work of James Fowler (1980, 1981, 1983, 1996)—a great influence in the development of Jamieson's model—does provide some more specific reflection upon how churches may facilitate personal faith journeys. He explores three characteristics of communities which nurture—rather than stifle or suppress—this growth journey: (1) re-envisioning the nature of religious truth, (2) a lack of fear of the intimacy of conflict and the inevitable presence of doubt and struggle, and (3) a climate of developmental expectation. More specifically, Fowler advocates the use of rites of passage, thresholds or milestones of the spiritual journey which churches can use to guide the maturation of individuals. He (1981, pp. 295–6) proposes a community which "will provide rites of passage and opportunities for vocational engagement that call forth the gifts and emergent strengths of each stage of faith" as well as "help for people in naming and clarifying the shape of their callings and challenges, in the community and the wider world, at each stage of their faith growth." Furthermore, church history (not to mention Christian Scriptures) provides a plentiful array of resources for the more developed stages of the Christian life, from Augustine to Martin Luther to Brother Lawrence. Church leaders can encourage their congregants to see themselves as followers in their footsteps. Many churches, JV included, are longing for a wider and fuller understanding of the Christian life than the one with which they were educated. To better realize this, a wider and fuller spectrum of Christian resources must be consulted.

However, a problem may emerge when reflecting upon this challenge for Christian education. Theology does not easily lend itself to fixed or formulaic notions of Christian maturity. Generating a "recipe" for spiritual growth from theological sources often seems incommensurable with the genre of those sources. It may even be posed that the question itself is misleading. For instance, reflection upon the appropriateness of an individual orientation to growth and maturity may reveal ways in which such a narrow focus may not be theologically faithful.

A helpful contrast may be found in considering the parallels between JV's dilemma and that of the current cultural situation. JV's "If not [practice or belief], then what? And why—on what basis?" tension illustrates it well. JVers were in agreement that maturity was not a certain set of superficial habits or abilities, but seemed unsure about what it was specifically or how to go about learning what it was. Similarly, recent cultural trends have also welcomed difference and sought to undermine the vision of an ideal rational self and a perfected society. Without the legitimating force of a common vision of progress, contemporary society tends to offer little or no authority for legitimating acceptable behavior. As a result, reflection on Christian education is not less important, but is needed even more, though it will inevitably be done in different ways. This congregational study highlights the necessity of reencountering the bases on which discipleship occurs, and relocates the Christian education emphasis from methods and tactics of formation to a reappraisal of its ultimate goals.

Perhaps the most pertinent resemblance of JV and similar churches' dilemmas to that of the contemporary western situation is the lack of a clear teleology, or ultimate vision of the future. Bereft of a grand metanarrative, local cultures and groups have been forced to develop their own vision of a preferred future from within, from their own resources. Since JV were a self-proclaimed experimental project for the emerging church, a natural question to consider is the ways in which JV constructed (or neglected to construct) a teleology to authenticate their existence and give direction to their activities. Apart from a clear self-identity of "different-ness", JV were struggling to find direction for reconstructing something new in relation to that from which they wished to be differentiated, much like liminal groups often do. It may be a reasonable suggestion that many churches are, or soon will be, undergoing a similar tension related to their teleological vision, or lack thereof.

Yet the Church cannot settle for a lack of teleology. Churches will need to first realize that the Christian tradition does not provide a timeless, universal model of growth and maturity. Instead, it promotes an awareness and appreciation of the ways in which Christians throughout biblical and post-biblical history have sought to respond to their cultural settings, sometimes well and other times poorly. At its best, the Church has not uncritically conformed to the notions of acceptable behavior in their situation, but exhibited an alternative lifestyle faithful to their understanding of what God required of them. At its worst, the Church has adopted the worst aspects of its culture and used its theological resources to ratify these values. Consequently, there exists not only a need for developing a unique and different vision for how to live in its surroundings, but also a critical suspicion of the faith community's interpretation of this vision.

More specifically, theological reflection may choose to ask questions of biblical theology related to the progressive process of redemption, such as looking at Jewish history as an account of the nation of Israel's attempts to fulfill its task of being God's blessing to the world.[13] It may also look to systematic theology and christology to understand the richness of Jesus' vision of the kingdom of God and the Church's participatory role in it.[14] The New Testament churches may serve as case studies of communities learning how to carry on Jesus' tradition in the face of severe cultural obstacles and divisions from within. Church history may also inspire theological reflection upon the response of churches in many other cultural contexts. Churches today may not only learn from the mistakes of their forefathers, so as not to repeat them, but also draw strength and wisdom from their successes. The clear imperative is that these other theological disciplines must increasingly direct the fruits of their studies in relation to the complexities and ambiguities of the current cultural situation, and propose a teleological vision which addresses these concerns.[15] As churches enhance and identify their understandings not merely of what an individual Christian is to be or how one is to behave, but more so of their collective role in God's future and present mission in the world, Christian growth and maturity (and, of course, the task of Christian education) will more readily align itself with those goals.

Consequently, practical theological reflection done well will cause a community of faith to see its mission as both a continuation of the Christian tradition and a transformative response to the needs of its situation. Maturity as a Christian may then be seen as effectiveness in this activity, and practical theology as a way of life—an expression of discipleship to Christ—rather than a dislocated cognitive inquiry. If situational analysis and theological reflection are combined in this way, it may produce churches which are, as JV also desire, disconnected from neither their culture nor their Christian vision. Christian education, if it takes seriously the questions which practical theology poses to it, may need to be reformulated with a central emphasis on correlating contextual challenges with theological identity, the experience of which is a dynamic journey of faith with many natural stages.

In addition to these other points of consideration, for emerging churches this comparable concept may particularly remind them of the necessity of continual growth and the readiness of their members for it. Since the movement as a whole views itself as growing out of or emerging from the limitations of evangelicalism,

---

13 See Brueggeman (1976, 1997).

14 In biblical scholarship since Albert Schweitzer, there has been an exciting rediscovery and renewed emphasis on the centrality of Jesus' teaching on the "kingdom of God". For discussions of Jesus and the kingdom of God, see Keck (1971), Wright (1996), Yoder (1994), and Rauschenbusch (1968).

15 For an eschatological discussion from one emerging church perspective, see Perriman (2006).

the temptation may exist to develop a view of spiritual maturity which is merely a differentiation from evangelicalism's norms. Liminal groups are between one thing and another. In the case of many emerging churches, a large number of their members are eager to move forward in their faith journeys, and without an intentionally reconstructive ethic, they are likely to become as disillusioned with insubstantial notions of maturity as they were with (what they perceived to be) the rigid or reductionistic criteria offered by evangelicalism. One of the dangers of the liminal state is that it may result in or be misconstrued with a relatively permanent state of outsider-hood, perhaps resembling what Jamieson (2002) labels marginal groups, whose focus is fixed on what they have left. The emerging church must counter this outsider state with robust yet flexible visions of maturity and ministry.

Communication with Contemporary Culture

A fourth comparative concept is that of communicating with contemporary culture, or, to put more broadly, relating to the Other. Attention to this concept arises from the high significance placed on this activity within Jacobsfield Vineyard, despite the relative ambiguity about what it entailed. In fact, communicating with contemporary culture was perhaps the most strongly felt value at JV. In the semi-structured interviews, a large majority of JVers identified their "central question" as pertaining to being "relevant" to their society. They consistently framed their *raison d'être* almost exclusively with an external or outward-looking focus. Since they viewed evangelical Christianity as lacking in this area, JV placed a high priority on experimentation in doing church for the purpose of better communicating to the culture around them those beliefs and values which make up who they are. This was most clearly seen in their attitudes towards evangelism. As noted in Chapter 3, one of the most commonly held values at JV was an avid rejection of "hard sell Christianity". I concluded that JV had a strong distaste for evangelicalism's evangelistic techniques, but they still wanted to communicate "the message of Christianity" despite the fact that they were unclear about how to communicate that message and exactly what that message is if it is more than praying a prayer for salvation in the afterlife.

For churches wishing to reflect on their communicative relationship to the culture in which they find themselves, a practical theological approach may bring them to pursuing the following lines of inquiry. First, this comparative concept necessitates a greater awareness of one's cultural situation. A good starting point for churches may be to consider the assumptions and presuppositions of post-Christian culture regarding the message of Christianity and the Church as an institution. With the decline of churches in the west, it is becoming increasingly obvious, as several authors[16] observe, that the Church (particularly in Britain) is

[16] For discussions, see Wuthnow (1997), Davie (1994), Brown (2000), and Woodhead and Heelas (2000).

now a marginalized organization while mainstream society is undoubtedly post-Christian. This trend cannot go unexamined; the landscape is extremely different than it was during Christendom, and these changes must be understood. Reflecting on one's relationship with the Other will cause churches to listen carefully, take responsibility for their own shortcomings, and consider how they can most appropriately speak from their new status in a very different society. One likely finding may be that while the west is growing increasingly irreligious, spiritual interest is rising. While interpersonal conversations are priceless, churches may also consult current discussions by Christian thinkers on the rising interest in spirituality such as those by Drane (2001, 2008), Ward (2002), Sweet (1999), Rabey (2001), and Davie (1994). Churches that recognize the spiritual journey already occurring in people's lives will likely have an advantage in their attempts to communicate with their communities. In practice, this heightened awareness of the stance of post-Christian culture to the message of Christianity will best be achieved through personal interaction, particularly the habit of intensive and nonjudgmental listening. Communication is not something done to or for others, but with them.

An insightful aside from the JV research may be helpful. One Sunday evening in late September 2003, I shared a meal with a young married couple from JV. While conducting a semi-structured interview (a pilot interview during the familiarization stage) with them afterwards, this twenty-something pair were asked to respond to a number of commonly used phrases in JV. Surprisingly, when the phrase "communication with culture" was mentioned, they both manifested a slight uneasiness with the term. The husband, who had endured a number of frustrating evangelical church experiences since his childhood, reacted negatively, saying it reminded him of "ranting", though he did concede that "it's important that we communicate with culture." His wife, who had not grown up in a Christian environment and demonstrated a remarkable absence of typical conservative evangelical presuppositions throughout the interview, replied by saying that her immediate assumption regarding the term was listening. "It's more about involving people and connecting them ..." she continued. "I prefer to think of 'merging culture' over and above 'emerging church'." She then paused and we all noted how interesting it was that for those raised in a Christian culture (in this case both her husband and the researcher), communication immediately prompted thoughts of saying or doing something to someone else. Yet for her, communicating ideas was naturally a two-way street, the primary activity of which was listening. Both JVers in this situation were obviously supportive of the notion of communicating with culture, but were hesitant to identify with any approach which appeared one-sided.

Another issue worth consideration when reflecting on communicating with or relating to the Other is the challenges and opportunities which the technological revolution has introduced. The past 15 years alone has revolutionized the manner in which people communicate. On one level, this period has drastically changed the actual medium of communication. Mobile phones are now widespread and taken for granted. The internet—via chat rooms, instant messaging, blogging, or simple emailing—omits the element of spoken words. Audio-visual technology has also taken great strides in disseminating and selling information. On another level, the kind of communication in which society participates is also undergoing drastic changes. Interpersonal contact is needed increasingly less; people are meeting and conversing electronically at rapidly higher rates. Despite its limitations, this also has its distinct advantages. The ease of communication makes the maintenance and development of relationships a simpler chore, and makes wider and more diverse relational networks feasible. There are fewer boundaries between cultures due to the internet, mass media, and international travel, causing interaction with those of different places and cultures more readily accessible. Recognizing the effects of the communication revolution is thus also very crucial. How churches respond in utilizing these factors in ways which support the church's mission will involve creative and imaginative uses of technology and a critical appraisal of the benefits and drawbacks of non-interpersonal mediums.

Another dimension in which churches may grow in awareness of contemporary culture is the shifting epistemological landscape.[17] Most scholars suggest that many people today reject the imagery of metanarratives and universal truth, pointing to the contextually dependent nature of truth and the power interests latent in claims to universal systems of thought. If such a truth is "out there", many contend, it is unknowable. This is particularly problematic for interpretations of the Christian faith based on rational argument and a comprehensive understanding of knowledge and truth. Consequently, the concept of communication with culture will also lead to a re-visitation of the nature of the Christian message. One current conversation which may prompt helpful reflection is the metamorphosis of what many have labeled modernism and its deconstructive offspring, often termed post-modernism. Historical theology may reveal some striking differences in the way Scriptures and the Christian faith were understood prior to the onset of modernism, and the way it has been viewed in other historical periods. Modernism championed rationality and legitimated truth by scientific criteria. Some authors argue that conservative Christianity has adopted this framework and expressed its truth claims within this paradigm, for better or for worse.[18]

Nancey Murphy (1996) contends that the Church reacted to the scientific criteria of the Enlightenment in two very different ways. Whereas pre-modern Christianity had relied upon the widespread belief in the mystic and the supernatural, now science became the foundation of all knowledge, seemingly cutting off the Christian faith at the knees. Questions were raised about the validity of a realm beyond the physical world, as well as a literal interpretation of Scripture. In response, liberals chose as their foundation universal religious experience, particularly as advocated by Schleiermacher. Conservatives then reacted against these liberal ideals, choosing instead to base their movement upon the foundation of the canonical Bible as the

---

17 For academic discussions of epistemology, see Greco and Sosa (1999).

18 For a wider breadth of perspectives on the intersection of theology and post-modernity, see Ward (2001).

inerrant and infallible Word of God. For Murphy and others such as Grenz and Franke (2001), the two liberal and evangelical camps in western Christianity were byproducts of differing ways of responding to modernism.

The existence of these paradigms is, of course, itself heavily contested. Though Lawton and many JVers were obviously attracted to the designations of modernism and post-modernism, other churches need not agree with the classifications. However, considering these categories may be a good conversation partner in coming to a greater awareness of their cultural situations. For instance, despite JV's self-described intentions to communicate to a post-modern world, many JVers still saw Christian truth through a very propositional lens (even if questioning those propositions was an acceptable practice); as a result, their experimentation often centered on pragmatic means of presenting rational truths about God. When questioned about their experimental "edge", JVers often pointed to their pleasing music style during worship times, Lawton's accessible Christian language during sermons, or the non-threatening atmosphere which they created for newcomers to Sunday meetings. When Lawton occasionally attempted to introduce the notion of an "alternative basis for living" as an understanding of the gospel, JVers were able to repeat his definition, but exhibited little ability to relate this to their mission of communicating with culture. What then might it mean to communicate Christianity to contemporary culture? Whether or not one interprets cultural shifts through the lenses of modernity and post-modernity is not crucial, but it is essential to be aware of the manners in which cultural epistemologies modify and mediate the Church's understanding of the Christian tradition.

As a result, the concept of communicating with culture will entail not only how and to whom the Church is to communicate, but also a critical encounter with the nature of Christian truth. Is it to be held as universal? Is it to be considered propositional or embodied? What role do skepticism and uncertainty play? Does a congregation's epistemological stance conflict with those with whom it aims to communicate? To what extent can a church claim absolute knowledge of the nature of God and the world? Does proclamation of the gospel imply an assertion of such a metanarrative? These tensions, experienced at JV and undoubtedly in many other settings, highlight the need for the discipline of practical theology to give greater attention to them. Churches may learn from treatments such as the one offered by Graham (1996) in which she suggests that post-modern theologies will need to emphasize the provisionality and strategic value of truth, reject foundationalist assumptions about reality, and ground truth-claims in the purposeful practices of faith communities. Recognizing the danger of compromising the Christian imperatives of hope and obligation and/or retreating into isolation, she suggests that theological truth-claims be seen as forms of *phronesis*, or forms of situated knowledge. Communication with culture, for Graham, entails the community of faith being drawn into dialogue with the Other and with the Church's own identity as a means of arriving at more effective practice. Graham's is one example of a way in which practical theology may help churches imagine ways of being authentically and effectively post-modern and Christian at the same time, while revealing as much need to listen to the Other as providing direction for speaking to the Other.

The biases of a post-Christian world, the technological revolution, and the epistemological landscape will also lead to theological reflection upon Christian resources. Primarily, it may center on the exploration of the theological imperative to communicate with culture and how this may correlate with the aforementioned challenges. Systematic theology may be asked to account for the various ways in which the people of God throughout biblical history have understood their obligation to represent God's blessing to the world. Special attention may be given to the ministry of Jesus in announcing the kingdom of God and the ongoing ministry of announcing this kingdom which he entrusted to the Church. While the kingdom of God is not easily quantifiable, churches which seek to more fully understand and embody it will reap great dividends. For churches with an external focus, such as the one found at JV, it will catalyze several more specific questions pertaining to what the gospel is and how it is to be announced. For those with a more internal focus, such a confrontation may serve to awaken a congregation to the priority of addressing the world beyond its walls. Since practical theology is focused upon helping churches become more critically faithful to their missional identity, an investigation into the mission of God as it relates to the Christian's obligation to announce or proclaim the kingdom of God will be crucial.

Another well from which to draw may be church history's findings on how churches in the past have handled their relationship with the secular Other. Their stories will not be viewed as formulas to be applied, but as comparative case studies from which lessons and insights (both helpful and unhelpful) can be drawn. While it may appear that the first-century Church's setting was far different than that of Christians in the Middle Ages or the Reformation, and certainly unlike the situation faced today, the dissimilarities should not discount comparison. If these religious ancestors can be seen as the carriers of one's own tradition who attempted to live faithful to that tradition in the circumstances confronting them at the time, much can be learned from the wisdom of church history. Reflecting on the concept of communication with culture ought not to overlook their stories, for they were engaged in the same sort of dialogue themselves.

Ultimately, there are no simplistic solutions for communicating with contemporary culture. Theological reflection on how to communicate the gospel may not produce a wealth of prescriptions, but it will encourage churches to keep their communicative action loyal to their theological imperative while remaining sensitive to their surrounding cultures. In recognizing the communication gap which exists between Christian churches and post-Christian culture, the temptation may exist to resolve this tension by conceding powerful elements of the Christian message. This is neither necessary nor helpful. While an honest engagement with the challenges of metanarratival truth may bring Christians to a more humble or nuanced announcement of their beliefs, it does not negate their imperative of proclamation. Regarding the perplexity about evangelism which JV and other congregations experience, practical theological reflection on the concept of communicating with or relating to the Other may choose to focus on effective ways of inviting others into the mission of God. With that understanding, appropriate practical means of communication can be evaluated and chosen. The choices congregations make in communicating with their surrounding culture may and will differ, but it is clear that in a cultural setting which is at best disinterested and at worst hostile to Christianity, carefully and critically reflecting on how to best handle this relationship will be an invaluable activity.

As for the emerging church, it may be said that due to the shared reasons behind its existence, emerging churches are relatively self-conscious of their situations, especially their sensitivity to the declining state of Christianity and the challenges of contemporary culture. Consequently, for the emerging church the comparable concept of communication with contemporary culture will not be one which confronts their apathy, but one which presses them to thoughtfully nurture lines of two-way conversation with the world around them and, potentially, challenge other Christian churches with the results of this dialogue. While JV, of course, would definitely benefit from more situational analysis, the JV congregational study seems to show that their greatest need may be correlating their theological resources with this cultural situation to which they desire to be relevant. JV cannot be accused of being isolationists. They were very keen to correlate Christianity with their culture; how this was to be done was an unresolved and sometimes contentious matter, and the same may be true of other emerging churches. Therefore, one recommendation (particularly for the emerging church, but also for all churches) is the envisioning of theologically-faithful metaphors for and the training of skills in correlating theology with the needs of their situation. In other words, these emerging churches may be encouraged to draw upon their theology in the creation of commonly accepted praxis for "being relevant". In the JV situation, when congregants were asked to explain why a certain practice (for example, worship style, ancient-future faith observances, or atmosphere in Sunday services) was relevant or not relevant, they rarely made recourse to theological language or concepts, but instead justified (or found fault) based on personal tastes or preferences. If churches wish to align themselves with the mission of God, efforts of "relevance" need to find their footing in some image or understanding of God's mission in the world. In their zeal to correct the errors and balance the extremes of their religious parents which have (in their perception) contributed to the marginalized status of Christianity in society, emerging churches must not lose the imperative to relate to their culture on theological terms.

Challenges of Reconstruction

A fifth comparable concept arising from the JV congregational study is the challenges of reconstruction. In Chapter 4, I proposed that JV's central question was identifying some criteria, or consensus of approach, for going about the process of replacing their evangelical and secular-world identities with something different though not entirely disconnected. JV therefore highlights not only the necessity of reconstruction, but the inevitable complexity and difficulty of such a process. This concept is especially pertinent not only for Jacobsfield Vineyard, but also for many other EPC and post-EPC churches undergoing the tensions of deconstructing their traditional practices and/or beliefs. Obviously, this notion of reconstruction is implicit in each of the comparable concepts discussed thus far; as a result, this section will devote itself to reflection not on the potential or desirable results of reconstruction, but on the difficulties and challenges of the process itself.

First, this concept can move across a variety of ecclesial contexts because reconstruction is inherent in the nature of change. When crisis—large or small—occurs, destabilization follows. And with destabilization comes the possibility of change, and change involves breaking down and building up. However, destabilization does not ensure positive change. It also creates the possibility for a variety of unhelpful responses. First, reconstruction may result in a reactionary, angry, or disillusioned response, characterized by defining oneself by what one is not, namely that group or identity which one has left. Churches such as JV and others affiliated with the emerging church movement who share disaffection with evangelicalism certainly face this danger, as highlighted by the descriptions of marginal churches provided by Jamieson. Second, there is also the temptation to partially resort to that which is most familiar, if only to achieve some semblance of definiteness. For example, this was observed toward the end of the fieldwork period as JV began to speak less and less of their "emerging church" identity and manifested and increasing amount of overtly evangelical characteristics in their Sunday services. Third, reconstruction may also be inadvertently left up to the individual, thus depriving churches of the process of communal dialogue and abandoning members to the limitations of their own perspectives. Surely imposed ideological homogeneity is not a preferable alternative, but attention must be given to the balance between these extremes. While there can be no final or ideal pattern for reconstruction, reflection on such tensions indicates a need for an intentional, critical, hopeful, and ongoing approach to reconstruction. Indeed, becoming skilled in the process of reconstruction and transitioning may be the most helpful learning point of all, for it will ensure a congregation's flexibility and guide it through the ever-changing situations which it confronts.

As a result, one helpful line of inquiry for churches reflecting on the challenges of reconstruction may be exploring the nature of Christian tradition. This is not merely a consultation with biblical and extra-biblical resources, but rather a consideration of how faithfulness to tradition requires change; reconstruction is not something aided by the Christian tradition, but something demanded by it in order to preserve its integrity. Churches may more fully understand its nature by educating themselves with stories from church history in which members of the Christian tradition were forced to deconstruct their practices and understandings of their faith in order to be more critically faithful. Contemporary churches may then consider to what extent these churches effectively or ineffectively responded to their challenges. What voices did they involve? Was the process chaotic or complex? What difficulties did they face? From this point, churches can begin to see themselves as faced with the similar challenge of continually reconstructing the life of discipleship in their own setting. Furthermore, academic theologians are encouraged to speak in such a way that promotes and resources this communal dialogue, recognizing that the task of preserving the Christian tradition is performed by local churches, and is a fundamental activity of the Christian life.

Adeptness at reconstruction may have a couple prerequisites. First, churches may need to sustain the tension between settling on a firm identity and permitting uncertainty. Some congregants will undoubtedly desire the security of something definite, and will likely lean toward fixed identities. The danger here is hastiness and a closed cycle of reinterpretation. On the other hand, other congregants, aware of the extreme complexities of their world and their faith, will never be satisfied with final interpretations, and rightfully so. However, unending dialogue may paralyze action and suspend tangible transformation. Faith communities will thus face the challenge of constructing new practices and beliefs which are self-consciously vulnerable and likely to be deconstructed and revised at a later time. On a closely related wavelength, another tension which must be sustained is the inevitable collision of congregants at many different stages of their faith journeys, not to mention congregants representing a myriad of perspectives. Complete consensus is not feasible, nor is it desirable, but practical theological dialogue of the sort advocated here will demand that members of faith communities not only agree to disagree, but also find reason to associate and work alongside one another.

Since deconstruction and reconstruction are such fundamental characteristics of the emerging church, its practitioners are encouraged to give ample attention to these challenges, and to model this activity for other churches. Fortunately, its participants are likely to be very keen to undergo the process, but eagerness does not guarantee proficiency. The JV congregational study highlights the fact that there is a large gap between deciding to move away from something and actually reconstructing something theologically faithful and culturally relevant to take its place. The route is difficult, and then begins all over again. Emerging church leaders would do well to "warn" their congregations that the journey is complicated and strenuous, one that demands patience, cooperation, and tolerance. How the emerging church navigates the waters of reconstruction will determine its destiny and how it will be judged many years from now. Ideally, it will be an excellent model for other churches' journeys, even if their eventual conclusions are radically different.

Ultimately, this challenge of reconstruction returns to the activity of practical theology. The intent of contemporary practical theology is to provide helpful patterns and voices which may assist churches in the ongoing task of deconstruction and reconstruction. Beginning and ending with ecclesial praxis, practical theology moves to situational analysis and theological reflection, generates more critically faithful praxis, and then begins again. It is not an occasional medicine for crises, but a continuous movement which must be sustained. Consequently, the challenge of reconstruction could also be seen as the challenge of doing practical theology well.

Recommendations for Practical Theological Research

These five comparable concepts primarily apply to other ecclesial contexts, offering transformative points of reflection and further lines of inquiry. Since the starting point of the study was practical theology, in this final section I will address three ways in which the Jacobsfield Vineyard congregational study may speak to the field of practical theology.

The Effectiveness of Congregational Studies

First, this book has attempted to demonstrate the helpfulness of a congregational study as an expression of practical theological inquiry and the necessity of more similar ventures. As I demonstrated in Chapter 1, congregational studies have and will still be used for other disciplinary inquiries, but they are an excellent and useful outworking of practical theology. It is hoped that the congregational study will be a vehicle for practical theology on two levels.

On one level, it is a fruitful endeavor for practitioners leading and operating within local churches. This congregational study has intended to show the transformative potential of the practical theological cycle, the accessibility of ethnographic methods, and the helpfulness of identifying and addressing new and challenging questions. Congregations may undergo similar processes of bringing their own life under investigation, motivated by the vision of being more critically faithful to the mission of God in their local settings. Ideally, a congregational study could become less a one-time investigation and more a way-of-being for a local church: a continuous, synergistic movement between situational analysis and theological reflection leading to ever-renewing praxis.

On another level, academic practical theologians are encouraged to make greater use of congregational studies in their research. Since the theological interpretation of particular situations not only yields insight for the specific situation studied, but also for many other situations, deepening the well of available congregational studies will give theological educators and researchers a much richer resource from which to draw. The disadvantage to a congregational study is that it does not typically begin with and focus on the exploration of a specific issue (for example, poverty, charismatic gifts, or leadership), but this can also be its greatest strength. By allowing questions and concerns to arise from situations as opposed to placing theoretical frameworks upon them as Chapter 1's critique of Hopewell (1987) highlighted, practical theologians are forced to consider questions other than their own. Practical theological research which remains closely connected to local situations will thus engender a mutually dependent and mutually beneficial relationship between practical theologians in the churches and those in universities.

The Emerging Church

A second recommendation for future research pertains to the nascent, evolving movement labeled the "emerging church". It is evident from this congregational study that the emerging church is: (1) a diverse and heterogeneous network which no single church can fully represent and (2) an intriguing group with much to tell the wider Church. While the emerging church network manifests informal connections and a similar story of discontent and experimentation, the ways in which they have outworked those sentiments have been very diverse. As a result, if the wider Church is to take them seriously and bring them more fully to the table of dialogue, more research will need to be done on congregations identifying with this network. The JV congregational study, by providing rich detail and authentic characters, may help bring credibility to the emerging church movement, thus serving as a contribution to securing and strengthening its place at the table.

Another reason that practical theology requires more research on the emerging church is for the emerging church's own benefit. JV's story may make explicit various aspects of their own life of which they were unaware. For instance, most emerging church congregants may be relatively conscious of their disaffection with expressions of evangelical Christianity; they may not, however, be as conscious of their own potential confusions over using the Bible, contradictions in their practices of worship, or a lack of consensus regarding Christian maturity. They will likely be encouraged by a church with a parallel story, but also concerned with the tensions which result from that story. Since the emerging church finds its shape in informal conversational networks spanning nations and continents (as opposed to a centralized organization), other formal studies of specific churches guided by ethnographic methods and a practical theological methodology may provide rich, intriguing detail which will enhance the current dialogue. Moreover, in giving voice to the many participants of a church, congregational studies may make known the perspectives of emerging church participants who would not normally voice themselves in these informal conversational networks. Future research on the emerging church will also need to be sensitive to the fact that, since it is composed of proactive agents of change, the emerging church is always mutating and reshaping itself. Therefore, any conclusions about these churches must be provisional and flexible.

Additionally, the emerging church draws attention to issues which may have been overlooked or neglected. Though these churches may not be a prototype of twenty-first century Christianity, their liminal features serve as helpful catalysts for contemplating issues of great significance for the future of the Church. In speaking of liminality, Turner (1982, p. 145) suggests that people or societies in a liminal phase are a "kind of institutional capsule or pocket which contains the germ of future social developments, of societal change." In short, liminal groups contain the seeds of what is to come, or at least point to what is to come. Congregational studies such as this one may prompt reflection on the tensions resulting from moving away from evangelical Christianity (while, as in JV's case, still retaining many of its features) and the confusions of intentional engagement with contemporary culture, such as the influence of post-modernity. In rapidly changing cultural contexts, the emerging church—regardless of how effective or ineffective their responses may be judged to be—is highlighting a set of concerns and issues which will be of vital importance to the Church in the upcoming decades. Of course, their preoccupation with such matters may blind them to other significant horizons, but the questions which they are asking cannot go unheard or unaddressed.

Posing Questions to Other Theological Disciplines

Consequently, a final recommendation is for a stronger partnership between practical theology and other theological disciplines in addressing the questions which emerge from congregational studies such as this. Churches, JV included, are eager to learn from theology if its findings are relevant for the challenges of their circumstances. Practical theology must not discourage or minimize the research of systematic, historical, biblical, or historical theology; instead, the opposite should be true. Practical theology should catalyze greater quantities and deeper explorations of these other theological fields because it will constantly bring new and challenging questions to their resources, such as the ones highlighted in previous sections. New insights will undoubtedly emerge; old understandings will be modified, re-appropriated, or discarded. The crucial task is greater cooperation among the theological disciplines in sharing and testing their findings, as well as the willingness of churches to be challenged and changed by their encounters with these findings. The uniting vision amongst these disciplines, practical theology included, is the creation and ongoing reformation of communities of faith which critically and faithfully participate in the mission of God in the world, and in their local settings.

Appendix A:
JV Demographic Survey

The information below was given to participants as a separate sheet of paper to keep as reference. The latter page was collected in the manner outlined in Part Two, B.4.

Jacobsfield Vineyard Survey

Thank you for showing an interest in this project. Please read this information carefully before deciding whether or not to participate. If you decide not to take part, there will be no disadvantage to you of any kind and I thank you for considering my request. Engaging in this survey is an indication of your willingness to participate and that you understand that:

1. your participation in the project is entirely voluntary;
2. you are free to withdraw at any time;
3. the results of the project may be published but anonymity will be preserved.

This information will be used as part of my doctoral research, to be presented in the form of a doctoral thesis for a Ph.D. degree. The research is exploring how local churches might best respond to the challenges of our post-modern cultural situation. Results of this project may be published but any data included will in no way be linked to any specific participant. You are most welcome to request a copy of the results of the project should you wish. If you have any questions about my project, either now or in the future, please feel free to contact me:

Cory Labanow
38 Astbury Road
Peckham, London
SE15 2NJ
020 7639 0332 or 07739 836719

Please tick one box per question, or write in the space provided.

1. Individual Information:

Year in which you were born: 19_____

Gender: □ Male □ Female

Present marital status: □ Never married □ Cohabiting in a de-facto relationship
□ Separated or divorced □ Remarried □ Widowed
□ Married

2. How long have you been involved at Jacobsfield Vineyard?
_______ years _______ months

3. How frequently do you attend Sunday meetings here?
□ Hardly ever
□ Less than once a month
□ Once monthly
□ 2 times monthly
□ 3 times monthly
□ Usually every week
□ I am visiting and do not attend regularly

4. Are you regularly involved in other Jacobsfield Vineyard activities or ministries besides Sunday, such as home groups, Jacobsfield Furniture Project, Wendy House, mentor groups, or others?
□ Yes □ No If "Yes", how often (on average)?
□ Monthly
□ 2–3 times a month
□ Once per week
□ 2–3 times per week or more

5. Previous church experience:

Years (e.g. 1990–96)	*Best Label* (liberal, evangelical, charismatic, Anglican, Baptist, or others)	Reason(s) moved
□ No significant previous church experience.		

Appendix B:
Semi-structured Interview Questionnaire

The first page was either discussed orally directly prior to the interview or sent to the interviewee(s) ahead of time. The results of the second form, the questionnaire, are outlined in Chapter 3.

Information Sheet for Interview Participants

Thank you for showing an interest in this project. Please read this information carefully before deciding whether or not to participate. If you decide not to take part, there will be no disadvantage to you of any kind and I thank you for considering my request. Engaging in this interview is an indication of your willingness to participate and that you understand that:

1. your participation in the project is entirely voluntary;
2. you are free to withdraw from the interview at any time;
3. the results of the project may be published but anonymity will be preserved.

This project is being undertaken as part of the requirements for a Ph.D. The research is exploring how local churches might best respond to the challenges of our post-modern cultural situation. This information will be used as part of my doctoral research, to be presented in the form of a doctoral thesis. Results of this project may be published but any data included will in no way be linked to any specific participant. You are most welcome to request a copy of the results of the project should you wish. If you have any questions about my project, either now or in the future, please feel free to contact me:

Cory Labanow
38 Astbury Road
Peckham, London
SE15 2NJ
020 7639 0332 or 07739 836719

Part One: Basic Reflections on Jacobsfield Vineyard

Personal Information: Age, Marital Status, Duration and Frequency of Involvement, Previous Church Experience.

1. How did you come to JV?

2. Why are you here? i.e. What needs are being met by JV?

3. Have you ever experienced a definitive crisis in your faith (or, identity as a Christian)? If yes, how has JV been involved?

4. Reflect on:
   a. the use of elements of historical Christianity, such as observance of the Christian calendar, creeds, prayers, and other ancient practices
   b. worship
   c. the use of the Bible
   d. the phrase 'doubts and questions'

Part Two: Analysis of Deeper Issues

5. What is 'spiritual maturity' at JV? How does it relate to 'messy spirituality'?

6. Where would JV be on a 'church map'? Would you describe it as a Vineyard church, an evangelical church, an emerging church, none of those, all of those, or something completely different?

7. Is there a central issue JV are wrestling with or a question they are striving to answer?

8. Sometimes Matt uses the phrase 'alternative basis for living'. What does that phrase mean to you?

9. My last question is about 'power'. Part of my research focuses on the way in which power is misused and used rightly. Is there any difference in the way power is used at JV versus the way in which it is used, for instance, in the business world or wider society?

Works Cited

Ammerman, N., 1987. *Bible believers: fundamentalists in the modern world.* New Brunswick: Rutgers University Press.

———, 1997. *Congregation and community.* New Brunswick: Rutgers University Press.

———, 1998. Culture and identity in the congregation. In: Ammerman, N.T., Carroll, J.W., Dudley, C.S. and McKinney, W. eds, 1998. *Studying congregations: a new handbook.* Nashville: Abingdon Press.

Ammerman, N.T., Carroll, J.W., Dudley, C.S. and McKinney, W. eds, 1998. *Studying congregations: a new handbook.* Nashville: Abingdon Press.

Anderson, W.T., 1992. *Reality isn't what it used to be: theatrical politics, ready-to-wear religion, global myths, primitive chic and other wonders of the postmodern world.* San Francisco: Harper.

———, 1995. *The truth about the truth: de-confusing and re-constructing the postmodern world.* New York: G.P. Putnam's Sons.

Aristotle, (n.d.). *Nicomachean ethics.* Translated by D.P. Chase, 1998. Mineola: Dover.

Atkinson, P., Coffey, A. and Delomont, S., 2003. *Key themes in qualitative research: continuities and change.* New York: AltaMira Press.

Atkinson, P. and Hammersley, M., 1998. Ethnography and participant observation. In: N.K. Denzin and Y.S. Lincoln eds, 1998. *Strategies of qualitative inquiry.* London: Sage.

Ballard, P., 1986. The challenge of sociology. In: P. Ballard ed., 1986. *The foundations of pastoral studies and practical theology.* Cardiff: HOLI.

———, 1999. Practical theology as the theology of practice. In: F. Schweitzer and J.A. Van der Ven eds, 1999. *Practical theology: international perspectives.* Frankfurt: Peter Lang.

Ballard, P. and Pritchard, J., 1996. *Practical theology in action: Christian thinking in the service of church and society.* London: SPCK.

Banks, R., 1999. *Reenvisioning theological education: exploring a missional alternative to current models.* Grand Rapids: Eerdmans.

Barth, K., 1963. *Evangelical theology.* London: Weidenfield and Nicholson.

Bellah, R. *et al.*, 1985. *The habits of the heart.* Berkeley: University of California Press.

Berger, P., 1961. *The noise of solemn assemblies.* Garden City, NY: Doubleday.

Bernstein, R.J., 1971. *Praxis and action.* Philadelphia: University of Pennsylvania Press.

Blumer, H. *Symbolic interactionism: perspective and method.* Englewood Cliffs: Prentice-Hall.

Boff, L. and Boff, C., 1987. *Introducing liberation theology.* Tunbridge Wells: Burns and Oates.

Bogdan, R. and Taylor, S.J., 1975. *Introduction to qualitative research methods.* New York: John Wiley and Sons.

Bosch, D., 1991. *Transforming mission: paradigm shifts in theology of mission.* Maryknoll: Orbis.

Brierley, P. ed., 2003. *UK Christian handbook religious trends no.4 – 2003/2004.* London: Christian Research.

Brown, C.G., 2000. *The death of Christian Britain: understanding secularization: 1800–2000.* London: Routledge.

Browning, D., 1976. *The moral context of pastoral care.* Philadelphia: Westminster.

———, 1983a. Introduction. In: D. Browning ed., 1983. *Practical theology: the emerging field in theology.* New York: Harper and Row.

———, 1983b. Pastoral theology in a pluralistic age. In: D. Browning ed., 1983. *Practical theology: the emerging field in theology.* New York: Harper and Row.

———, 1983c. *Religious ethics and pastoral care.* Philadelphia: Fortress Press.

———, 1987. Practical theology and religious education. In: L.S. Mudge and J.N. Poling eds, 1987. *Formation and reflection: the promise of practical theology.* Philadelphia: Fortress Press.

———, 1991. *A fundamental practical theology: descriptive and strategic proposals.* Minneapolis: Fortress.

Brueggemann, W., 1976. *Living toward a vision: biblical reflections on shalom.* Philadelphia: United Church Press.

———, 1978. *The prophetic imagination.* Philadelphia: Fortress Press.

———, 1992. *Hopeful imagination: prophetic voices in exile.* London: SCM Press.

———, 1997. *Theology of the Old Testament: testimony, dispute, advocacy.* Minneapolis: Fortress Press.

Burkhart, J.E., 1983. Schleiermacher's vision for theology. In: D. Browning ed., 1983. *Practical theology: the emerging field in theology.* New York: Harper and Row.

Burnham, J., 2004. *Perspectives on The Passion of the Christ: religious thinkers and writers explore the issues raised by the controversial movie.* New York: Miramax Books.

Campbell, A., 2000. The nature of practical theology. In: J. Woodward and S. Pattison eds, 2000. *The Blackwell reader in pastoral and practical theology.* Oxford: Blackwell.

Campbell, C., 1987. *The romantic ethic and the spirit of modern consumerism.* Oxford: Blackwell.

Capps, D., 1983. *Life cycle theory and pastoral care.* Philadelphia: Fortress Press.

———, 1990. *Reframing: a new method in pastoral care.* Minneapolis: Fortress Press.

Carroll, J.W., Dudley, C.S. and McKinney, W. eds, 1987. *Handbook for congregational studies*. Nashville: Abingdon Press.

Carson, D.A., 2005. *Becoming conversant with the emerging church*. Grand Rapids: Zondervan.

Cartledge, M.J., 2003. *Practical theology: charismatic and empirical perspectives*. Carlisle: Paternoster Press.

Charmaz, K., 2000. Grounded theory: objectivist and constructivist methods. In: N.K. Denzin and Y.S. Lincoln eds, 2000. *Handbook of qualitative research*. 2nd ed. London: Sage.

Chopp, R.S., 1987. Practical theology and liberation. In: L.S. Mudge and J.N. Poling eds, 1987. *Formation and reflection: the promise of practical theology*. Philadelphia: Fortress Press.

Coffey, A. and Atkinson, P., 1996. *Making sense of qualitative data: complementary research strategies*. Thousand Oaks: Sage.

Colson, C., 2003. The postmodern crackup: from soccer moms to college campuses, signs of the end. *Christianity Today*, 47 (12).

Cracknell, K. and White, S.J., 2005. *An introduction to world methodism*. Cambridge: Cambridge University Press.

Crouch, A., 2004. The emergent mystique. *Christianity Today*, 48 (11).

D'Andrade, R.G., 1992. Afterword. In: R.G. Andrade and C. Strauss eds, 1992. *Human motives and cultural models*. Cambridge: Cambridge University Press.

Davie, G., 1994. *Religion in Britain since 1945*. Oxford: Blackwell.

Denzin, N.K., 1989. *The research act: a theoretical introduction to sociological methods*. 3rd ed. Englewood Cliffs: Prentice-Hall.

———, 1997. *Interpretive ethnography: ethnographic practices for the 21st century.* London: Sage.

Denzin, N.K. and Lincoln, Y.S. eds, 1998. *Strategies of qualitative inquiry*. London: Sage.

Douglas, M., 1982. *Natural symbols: explorations in cosmology*. New York: Pantheon.

Dowie, A., 2002. *Interpreting culture in a Scottish congregation*. New York: Peter Lang.

Drane, J., 2001. *The McDonaldization of the church: spirituality, creativity, and the future of the church*. Macon, GA: Smyth and Helwys.

———, 2008. *After McDonaldization: mission, ministry, and Christian discipleship in an age of uncertainty*. London: Grand Rapids: Baker Academic.

Driscoll, M. *et al.*, 2007. *Listening to the beliefs of emerging churches: five perspectives*. Grand Rapids: Zondervan.

Dudley, C.S. ed., 1983. *Building effective ministry: theory and practice in the local church*. San Francisco: Harper and Row.

Dutton, E.C., 2005. Crop-tops, hipsters and liminality: fashion and differentiation in two evangelical student groups. *Journal of Religion and Popular Culture*, 9.

———, 2007. "Bog off dog breath! You're talking pants!" Swearing as witness evangelism in student evangelical groups. *Journal of Religion and Popular Culture*, 16.

———, 2008. *Meeting Jesus at university: rites of passage and student evangelicals*. Aldershot: Ashgate.

Eade, J. and Sallnow, M.J. eds, 1991. *Contesting the sacred: the anthropology of Christian pilgrimage*. London: Routledge.

Emergent Village, 2005. Explore: the emergent story. *Emergent Village,* [Online]. Available at http://www.emergentvillage.com/Site/Explore/EmergentStory/index.htm. [Accessed 21 June 2005].

Emergent Village UK., 2005. The emergent story …. *Emergent Village UK*, [Online]. Available at http://www.emergent-uk.org. [Accessed 21 June 2005].

Farley, E., 1983. Theology and practice outside the clerical paradigm. In: D. Browning ed., 1983. *Practical theology: the emerging field in theology*. New York: Harper and Row.

———, 1987. Interpreting situations: an inquiry into the nature of practical theology. In: L.S. Mudge and J.N. Poling eds, 1987. *Formation and reflection: the promise of practical theology*. Philadelphia: Fortress Press.

———, 1988. *Theologia: the fragmentation and unity of theological education*. Philadelphia: Fortress Press.

Feeley-Harnik, G., 1995. Religion and food: an anthropological perspective. *Journal of the American Academy of Religion*, 63 (3).

Forrester, D.B., Can theology be practical? In: F. Schweitzer and J.A. Van der Ven eds, 1999. *Practical theology: international perspectives*. Frankfurt: Peter Lang.

Fowler, J.W., 1980. Future Christians and church education. In: T. Runyon ed., 1980. *Hope for the church*. Nashville: Abingdon.

———, 1981. *Stages of faith: the psychology of human development and the quest for meaning.* San Francisco: Harper and Row.

———, 1983. Practical theology and the shaping of Christian lives. In: D. Browning ed., 1983. *Practical theology: the emerging field in theology*. New York: Harper and Row.

———, 1987. The emerging new shape of practical theology. In: L.S. Mudge and J.N. Poling eds, 1987. *Formation and reflection: the promise of practical theology*. Philadelphia: Fortress Press.

———, 1996. *Faithful change: the personal and public challenges of postmodern life*. Nashville: Abingdon.

———, 1999. Practical theology and the social sciences. In: F. Schweitzer and J.A. Van der Ven. eds, 1999. *Practical theology: international perspectives*. Frankfurt: Peter Lang.

Friere, P., 1996. *Pedagogy of the oppressed.* Translated by M.M. Ramos, 1996. London: Penguin.

Frye, N., 1957. *Anatomy of criticism.* Princeton: Princeton University Press.

Gadamer, H., 1989. T*ruth and method.* 2nd ed. Translated by J. Weinsheimer and D.G. Marshall, 2003. New York: Continuum.

Garvin, H.R., ed., 1980. *Romanticism, modernism, postmodernism.* London: Bucknell University Press.

Geertz, C., 1973. *The interpretation of cultures.* New York: Basic Books, 1973.

Gergen, K., 1991. *The saturated self: dilemmas of identity in contemporary life.* New York: Basic Books.

Gerkin, C., 1984. *The living human document: revisioning pastoral counseling in a hermeneutical mode.* Nashville: Abingdon Press.

———, 1986. *Widening the horizons: pastoral responses to a fragmented society.* Philadelphia: Westminster Press.

———, 1997. *An introduction to pastoral care.* Nashville: Abingdon Press.

Glaser, B. and Strauss, A., 1967. *The discovery of grounded theory.* Chicago: Aldine Publishing.

Gonzales, J., 1985. *The story of Christianity, vol. 2: the reformation to the present day*. San Francisco: Harper.

Graham, E.L., 1996. *Transforming practice: pastoral theology in an age of uncertainty*. London: Mowbray.

———, 2000. Practical theology as transforming practice. In: J. Woodward and S. Pattison eds, 2000. *The Blackwell reader in pastoral and practical theology.* Oxford: Blackwell.

Greco, J. and Sosa, E. eds, 1999. *The Blackwell guide to epistemology.* Oxford: Blackwell.

Grenz, S.J. and Franke, J.R., 2001. *Beyond foundationalism: shaping theology in a postmodern context.* Louisville: Westminster John Knox.

Grierson, D., 1984. *Transforming a people of God.* Melbourne: Joint Board of Christian Education and New Zealand.

Guba, E.G. and Lincoln, Y.S., 1994. Competing paradigms in qualitative research. In: N.K. Denzin and Y.S. Lincoln eds, 1994. *Handbook of qualitative research.* Thousand Oaks: Sage.

Guder, D. ed., 1998. *The missional church: the people of God sent on a mission.* Grand Rapids: Eerdmans.

Guest, M.J., 2002. Negot*iating community: an ethnographic study of an evangelical church.* Lancaster: University of Lancaster Press.

Gutierrez, G., 1979. *A theology of liberation.* London: Marshall, Morgan and Scott.

Habermas, J., 1973. *Theory and practice.* Boston: Beacon Press.

Habgood, J., 1983. *Church and nation in a secular age.* London: Darton, Longman and Todd.

Hammersley, M., 1989. *The dilemma of qualitative method: Herbert Blumer and the Chicago tradition.* New York: Routledge.

Hammersley, M. and Atkinson, P., 1983. *Ethnography: principles in practice.* London: Tavistock.

Harvey, D., 1989. *The condition of postmodernity: an enquiry into the origins of cultural change*. Cambridge: Basil Blackwell.

Hauerwas, S., 1981. *A community of character: towards a constructive Christian social ethic.* Notre Dame: University of Notre Dame.

Hauerwas, S. and Willimon, W.H., 1989. *Resident aliens: life in the Christian colony*. Nashville: Abingdon.

Heidegger, M., 1969. *Identity and difference*. Translated by J. Stambaugh, 1969. New York: Harper and Row.

Heitink, G., 1999. Practical theology: an empirical-orientated approach. In: F. Schweitzer and J.A. Van der Ven eds, 1999. *Practical theology: international perspectives*. Frankfurt: Peter Lang.

Hill, M., 1973. *A sociology of religion.* London: Heinemann Educational.

Hiltner, S., 1958. *Preface to pastoral theology.* Nashville: Abingdon Press, 1958.

———, 2000. Meaning and importance of pastoral theology. In: J. Woodward and S. Pattison eds, 2000. *The Blackwell reader in pastoral and practical theology*. Oxford: Blackwell.

Hopewell, J., 1987. *Congregation: stories and structures*. Philadelphia: Fortress.

Hughes, G., 1991. *Swearing: a social history of foul language, oaths, and profanity in English*. Oxford: Blackwell.

Van Deusen Hunsinger, D., 1996. *Theology and pastoral counseling.* Grand Rapids: Eerdmans.

Hunter III, G.G., 2000. *The Celtic way of evangelism: how Christianity can reach the West ... again.* Nashville: Abingdon.

James, W., 1928. *Pragmatism: a new name for some old ways of thinking*. Reprint ed. New York: Longmans, Green and Co.

Jameson, F., 1998. *The cultural turn: selected writings on the postmodern 1983–1998.* London: Verso.

Jamieson, A., 2002. *A churchless faith: faith journeys beyond the churches*. London: SPCK.

Jenkins, T., 1999. *Religion in English everyday life: an ethnographic approach*. Oxford: Berghahn.

Keck, L., 1971. *A future for the historical Jesus: the place of Jesus in preaching and theology.* Nashville: Abingdon Press.

Kirkpatrick, C. Pierson, M. and Riddell, M., 2000. *The prodigal project: journey into the emerging church*. London: SPCK.

Kolb, R., 1991. *Confessing the faith: reformers define the church, 1530–1580*. St. Louis: Concordia Publishing House.

Lamb, M., 1982. *Solidarity with victims: toward a theology of social transformation*. New York: Crossroad.

Lartey, E., 2000. Practical theology as a theological form. In: J. Woodward and S. Pattison eds, 2000. *The Blackwell reader in pastoral and practical theology*. Oxford: Blackwell.

LeCompte, M.D. and Preissle, J. with Tesch, R., 1993. *Ethnography and qualitative design in educational research*. 2nd ed. Orlando: Academic Press.

Lobkowitz, N., 1967. *Theory and practice: the history of a Marxist concept, from Aristotle to Marx*. Notre Dame, Indiana: University of Notre Dame Press.

Loder, J.E., 1999. Normativity and context in practical theology. In: F. Schweitzer and J.A. Van der Ven eds, 1999. *Practical theology: international perspectives*. Frankfurt: Peter Lang.

Lyon, B. 2000. What is the relevance of congregational studies for pastoral theology? In: J. Woodward and S. Pattison eds, 2000. *The Blackwell reader in pastoral and practical theology. Oxford: Blackwell.*

Lyotard, J., 1984. *The postmodern condition: a report on knowledge*. Translated by G. Bennington and B. Massumi, 2001. Manchester: Manchester University Press.

Maresco, P., 2004. Mel Gibson's *The Passion of the Christ*: market segmentation, mass marketing and promotion, and the internet. *Journal of Religion and Popular Culture*, 7.

Martin, D., 1970. *A sociology of English religion*. London: Heinemann Educational Books.

Marty, M.E., 1981. *The public church: mainline, evangelical, Catholic*. New York: Crossroad.

McCann, D.P., 1981. *Christian realism and liberation theology*. Maryknoll: Orbis Books.

———, 1983. Practical theology and social action: or what can the 1980s learn from the 1960s? In: D. Browning ed., 1983. *Practical theology: the emerging field in theology*. New York: Harper and Row.

McCann, D.P. and Strain, C.R., 1990. *Polity and praxis: a program for American practical theology*. Lanham: University Press of America.

McEnery, T., 2006. *Swearing in English: blasphemy, purity and power from 1586 to the present*. London: Routledge.

McLaren, B., 2000. *The church on the other side*. Grand Rapids: Zondervan.

———, 2001. *A new kind of Christian: a tale of two friends on a spiritual journey*. San Francisco: Jossey-Bass.

———, 2003. *The story we find ourselves in: further adventures of a new kind of Christian*. San Francisco: Jossey-Bass.

———, 2007. *Everything must change: Jesus, global crises, and a revolution of hope*. Nashville: Thomas Nelson.

Metz, J.B., 1980. *Faith in history and society: toward a practical fundamental theology*. Translated by D. Smith, 1980. New York: Seabury Press.

Milbank, J., 1991. *Theology and social theory: beyond secular reason*. Cambridge, Mass.: Blackwell.

Miller, D.E., 1997. *Reinventing American Protestantism: Christianity in the new millenium*. London: University of California Press.

Moltmann, J., 1975. An open letter to José Míguez Bonino. *Christianity and Crisis*, 36.

Mudge, L.S. and Poling, J.N., 1987. Epilogue. In: L.S. Mudge and J.N. Poling eds, 1987. *Formation and reflection: the promise of practical theology*. Philadelphia: Fortress Press.

Murphy, N., 1996. *Beyond liberalism and fundamentalism: how modern and postmodern philosophy set the theological agenda*. Valley Forge: Trinity Press International.

Nipkow, K.E., 1999. Practical theology and contemporary culture – paradigms for present and future. In: F. Schweitzer and J.A. Van der Ven eds, 1999. *Practical theology: international perspectives*. Frankfurt: Peter Lang.

Ogden, S.M., 1986. *On theology*. Dallas: Southern Methodist University Press.

Ogletree, T.W., 1983. Dimensions of practical theology. In: D. Browning ed., 1983. *Practical theology: the emerging field in theology*. New York: Harper and Row.

Palmer, P.J., 1981. *The company of strangers: Christians and the renewal of America's public life*. New York: Crossroad.

Pattison, S., 1994. *Pastoral care and liberation theology*. Cambridge: Cambridge University Press.

———, 2000. Some straw for the bricks: a basic introduction to theological reflection. In: J. Woodward and S. Pattison eds, 2000. *The Blackwell reader in pastoral and practical theology*. Oxford: Blackwell.

Pattison, S. and Woodward, J., 1994. A vision of pastoral theology. *Contact*. Pastoral Monograph, 4.

———, 2000. An introduction to pastoral and practical theology. In: J. Woodward and S. Pattison eds, 2000. *The Blackwell reader in pastoral and practical theology*. Oxford: Blackwell.

Peirce, C.S., 1979. *Collected papers*. Cambridge, MA: Belknap.

Percy, M., 1996. *Words, wonders and power: understanding contemporary Christian fundamentalism and revivalism*. London: SPCK.

———, 1997. Sweet rapture: subliminal eroticism in contemporary charismatic worship. *Theology and Sexuality*, 6.

Perriman, A., 2006. *The coming of the Son of Man: New Testament eschatology for an emerging church*. Carlisle: Paternoster Press.

Rabey, S., 2001. *In search of authentic faith: how emerging generations are transforming the church*. Colorado Springs: Waterbrook.

Rahner, K., 1968. *Theology of pastoral action*. Translated by W.J. O'Hara, 1968. New York: Herder and Herder.

Ramsay, N.J., 1992. The congregation as a culture: implications for ministry. *Encounter*, 53.

Rauschenbusch, W., 1968. *The righteousness of the kingdom*. Nashville: Abingdon Press.

Redeker, M., 1973. *Schleiermacher: life and thought*. Translated by J, Wallhausser, 1973. Philadelphia: Fortress.

Ricoeur, P., 1967. *The symbolism of evil*. Boston: Beacon.

Riddell, M., 1998. *Threshold of the future*. London: SPCK.

Robson, C., 2002. *Real world research: a resource for social scientists and practitioner-researchers*. London: Blackwell.

Ryle, G., 1971. *Collected papers*. London: Hutchinson.

Saarinen, M.F., 1986. *The life cycle of a congregation.* Washington: Alban Institute.

Sardar, Z., 1997. *Postmodernism and the other: the new imperialism of western culture.* London: Pluto, 1997.

Schleiermacher, F.E., 1811. *Brief outline on the study of theology*. Translated by T.N. Tice, 1966. Richmond: John Knox.

Schreiter, R., 1985. *Constructing local theologies.* Maryknoll: Orbis Books.

———, 1998. Theology in the congregation: discovering and doing. In: N.T. Ammerman, J.W. Carroll, C.S. Dudley, and W. McKinley eds, 1998. *Studying congregations: a new handbook.* Nashville: Abingdon Press.

Schweitzer, F., 1999. Interdisciplinary relationships and unity. In: F. Schweitzer and J.A. Van der Ven eds, 1999. *Practical theology: international perspectives.* Frankfurt: Peter Lang.

Silverman, D., 1993. *Interpreting qualitative data: methods for analyzing talk, text, and interaction.* London: Sage.

Southcott, E.W., 1956. *The parish comes alive.* London: Mowbray.

Spradley, J.P., 1980. *Participant observation.* London: Harcourt Brace Jovanovich.

Stokes, A. and Roozen, D., 1991. The unfolding story of congregational studies. In: C. Dudley, J. Carroll, and J. Wind eds, 1991. *Carriers of faith: lessons from congregational studies.* Louisville: Westminster John Knox, 1991.

Strauss, A. and Corbin, J., 1990. *Basics of qualitative research: grounded theory procedures and techniques.* London: Sage.

Stringer, M.D., 1999. *On the perception of worship: the ethnography of worship in four Christian congregations in Manchester.* Birmingham: University of Birmingham Press.

———, 2001. Introduction: theorizing faith. In: E. Arweck and M.D. Stringer eds, 2001. *Theorizing faith: the insider/outsider problem in the study of ritual.* Birmingham: University of Birmingham.

Sweet, L., 1999. *Soul tsunami* Grand Rapids: Zondervan..

Swinton, J., 2000. *From Bedlam to Shalom: towards a practical theology of human nature, interpersonal relationships, and mental health care.* New York: Peter Lang.

Swinton, J. and Mowat, H., 2006. *Practical theology and qualitative research.* London: SCM Press.

Thurneyson, E., 1962. *A theology of pastoral care.* Atlanta: John Knox Press.

Tillich, P., 1967. *Systematic theology: three volumes in one.* Chicago: University of Chicago Press.

Tomlinson, D., 1996. *The post-evangelical.* London: SPCK.

Tracy, D., 1975. *Blessed rage for order: the new pluralism in theology.* New York: Seabury Press.

———, 1981. *The analogical imagination.* New York: Crossroad.

———, 1983. Foundations of practical theology. In: D. Browning ed., 1983. *Practical theology.* San Francisco: Harper and Row.

———, 1987. Practical theology in the situation of global pluralism. In: L.S. Mudge and J.N. Poling eds, 1987. *Formation and reflection: the promise of practical theology*. Philadelphia: Fortress Press.

Triandis, H., 1995. *Individualism and collectivism*. Oxford: Westview Press.

Turner, V., 1969. *The ritual process: structure and anti-structure.* London: Routledge.

———, 1974. *Dramas, fields, and metaphors: symbolic action in human society.* Ithaca: Cornell University Press.

———, 1982. *From ritual to theatre: the human seriousness of play*. New York City: Performing Arts Journal Publications.

United Kingdom, 2004. *National Statistics Online: Census 2001,* [Online]. Available at: http://www.statistics.gov.uk/census2001/profiles/printV/00BF-A.asp. [Accessed 27 July 2004].

Van der Ven, J.A., 1999. An empirical approach to practical theology. In: F. Schweitzer. and J.A. Van der Ven eds, 1999. *Practical theology: international perspectives*. Frankfurt: Peter Lang.

Van Gennep, A., 1960. *The rites of passage*. Translated by M.B. Vizedom and G.L. Caffee, 1960. Chicago: University of Chicago Press.

Van Maanen, J., 1982. Fieldwork on the beat. In: J. Van Maanen, J.M. Dabbs, and R.R. Faulkner., 1982. *Varieties of qualitative research*. Beverly Hills: Sage.

Veling, T.A. and Groome, T.H., 1996. *Living in the margins: intentional communities and the art of interpretation.* New York: Crossroad.

Wagner, C.P., 1976. *Your church can grow*. Glendale: Regal.

Ward, C.K., 1961. *Priests and people: a study in the sociology of religion.* Liverpool: Liverpool University Press.

Ward, G. ed., 2001. *The Blackwell companion to postmodern theology*. Oxford: Blackwell.

Ward, P., 2002. *Liquid church*. Carlisle: Paternoster Press.

Webber, R., 1999. *Ancient-future faith: rethinking evangelicalism for a postmodern world.* Grand Rapids: Baker.

———, 2002. *The younger evangelicals: facing the challenges of the new world.* Grand Rapids: Baker.

Wheeler, B.G., 1983. Focus on the congregation: a look to the future. In: C.S. Dudley ed., 1983. *Building effective ministry: theory and practice in the local church*. San Francisco: Harper and Row.

Wind, J.P., 1993. *Constructing your congregation's story.* Minneapolis: Augsburg Fortress.

Wink, W., 1984. *Naming the powers: the language of power in the New Testament.* Philadelphia: Fortress.

Winter, G., 1961. *The suburban captivity of the churches.* Garden City, NY: Doubleday.

Wolcott, H.F., 1994. *Transforming qualitative data: description, analysis, and interpretation.* London: Sage.

Woodhead, L. and Heelas, P. eds, 2000. *Religion in modern times*. Malden, Mass.: Blackwell.

Woodhead, L. Guest, M. and Tusting, K., 2004. Congregational studies: taking stock. In: M. Guest, K. Tusting, and L. Woodhead eds, 2004. *Congregational studies in the UK: Christianity in a post-Christian context*. Burlington: Ashgate.

Wright, N.T., 1996. *Jesus and the victory of God: Christian origins and the question of God*. London: SPCK.

———, 2000. *The Challenge of Jesus*. London: SPCK.

Wuthnow, R., 1997. *The crisis in the churches: spiritual malaise, fiscal woe*. Oxford: Oxford University Press.

Yaconelli, M., 2001. *Messy spirituality: Christianity for the rest of us*. London: Hodder and Stoughton.

Yoder, J.H., 1994. *The politics of Jesus*. Grand Rapids: Eerdmans.

Index

Abductive reasoning 102–3
Acceptance 51, 59, 69, 78, 81–2, 87, 99, 109–12, 114
Alternative basis for living 64, 67, 71, 112, 120, 132
Ammerman, Nancy 26, 29, 44
Ancient-future faith (*see also* “Christian calendar observances”) 52, 65, 80, 96–7, 122
Applied theology 8, 10–11, 17
Aristotle 9, 15–16, 19, 23
Atkinson, Paul 31, 42, 102–3
Authority 29, 60, 65, 71, 80–81, 104

Ballard, Paul 8, 14, 22
Barth, Karl 12
Belonging 63–4, 68, 78–9, 85
Berger, Peter 25
Bible, the 2, 4, 6, 10, 29, 46, 49, 50, 59, 62, 67, 69–70, 73, 83–5, 87, 97, 105–6, 108, 112, 119, 126, 132
Biblical studies/theology 10, 104, 108, 112, 116, 123, 127
Blumer, Herbert 101, 103
Brierly, Peter 7, 38, 76
Browning, Don 10–11, 16–18, 21–2, 27–8, 33, 35–6, 42
Burkhart, John 10–11

Campbell, Alastair 10, 12
Candle Mass 85–6
Central theological question 36–7, 52, 59, 67, 70, 77, 87, 91–2, 100, 104, 117, 122
Christian calendar observances (*see also* “Ancient-future faith”) 47, 50, 67–9, 84–6, 96, 122, 132
Christian education 113–16
Christology 112, 116
Church Ministry Centre 50
Church planting 6–8, 37–8, 42, 51–2, 62, 68, 91, 95

Churches
- Anglican 47, 54–6, 70, 130
- Baptist 37, 47, 54–5, 67, 130
- Evangelical-pentecostal-charismatic (EPC) 59–60, 76–7, 91, 97, 109, 123

Coffey, Amanda 102–3
Communication
- Means of 27, 32, 119
- Of Christian message with secular culture i, 1, 17, 62, 72–3, 79, 86–91, 104, 117–22

Congregational study
- Applicability to other contexts 101–4, 109, 125–7
- Examples 26–9
- Historical development 25–7
- Relationship to ethnography 31–4
- Relationship to practical theology 29–31, 34–6
- Research 41–2

Consumerism 3, 61, 71, 78, 106, 111–12
Correlation (theologically) 12–13, 16, 18, 20–21, 23–4, 31, 35, 113, 116, 121–2
Critical faithfulness 22–3, 103, 114
Culture
Congregational 26–7, 22, 26–7, 29
- Definition 32–3
- Secular/contemporary i, 12, 30, 34–5, 56, 59, 62–5, 69–70, 76–8, 84, 87–92, 97–8, 104, 106, 111–12, 116–21, 127

Data collection
- Fieldwork notes 41, 43–5
- Interviews
  - Informal interviews 44–5, 71–2, 110
  - Semi-structured interviews 44–5, 52, 59, 61, 66–71, 73–4, 78, 80–81, 83–5, 87, 92, 94, 96, 111, 114, 118, 131

Methods 43–5
Survey 31, 43–6, 53–7, 67–8, 74, 78, 110, 129
Deconstruction 83, 99, 111, 114, 119, 123–4
Demographic survey (*see* "Data collection")
Demography
Jacobsfield 56–7
Jacobsfield Vineyard 31, 44–5, 53–57, 67, 74, 78, 129
Discipleship 9, 22, 36, 69, 73, 77, 84–5, 115–16, 124,
Disillusioned Followers 60, 76, 83
Doctrine 9–10, 30, 59, 76–7, 84, 106
Doubt 39–40, 64, 67, 69, 78, 81–2, 84, 90, 109, 111, 114, 132
Dowie, Al 28–9, 33
Dudley, Carl 26, 28

Ecclesiology 106
Effective history 20, 37, 39, 56
Elders 40, 51, 75–6, 80–81, 84
Emergent Village 5–6, 64, 73–4,
Emerging church
Challenges for 108–9, 113, 115–17, 122, 124
History of 2–6
Jacobsfield Vineyard's relationship to 1, 63–5, 67, 70, 72–4, 78, 92, 95, 97
Reflections on 104, 106
Relationship to liminality 106–8, 110, 115, 126
Relationship to other churches 109, 118, 123, 132
Research interests in 25, 42, 126
Enlightenment, the 2, 119
Epistemology 4, 11, 41, 102, 105, 119–21
Ethnography i, 31–4, 36, 42–4, 52, 101, 107, 125–6
Evangelicalism
As a whole 2, 4–5, 30, 42–3, 46, 51, 52, 54–5, 59, 62, 67, 70, 72–8, 85, 88–93, 97, 104–5, 107–9, 113–14, 116–18, 120, 122–3, 126, 130, 132
Opinions of 1
Pragmatic Evangelicals 2–4, 7, 46, 72, 77–8, 88, 93, 98, 109
Theology of 48
Traditional Evangelicals 2–4, 78, 109
Younger Evangelicals 2, 4, 42, 59–60, 64, 90, 93
Evangelism 1, 3–4, 7, 73, 75, 78, 87–90, 97, 99, 117, 121
Experimentation 2, 4–5, 49, 52, 60, 68, 72, 78, 84, 87, 94–7, 115, 117, 120, 126

Faith crisis 66–9, 79, 81, 111
Farley, Edward 8–10, 16, 19–20, 22, 33, 106
Fore-understandings 41–3, 56
Forrester, Duncan 8, 12, 14–16, 22
Fowler, James 9, 15–17, 22–3, 29, 106, 114
Frye, Northrop 27

Gadamer, Hans-georg 17–18, 20, 33, 41
Generalization 28, 101–3
Glaser, Barney 102–3
Graham, Elaine 21, 30, 120
Grierson, Denham 29
Grounded theory 102
Growth
Church Growth Movement 3, 5, 7, 50
Spiritual or personal 48, 59, 64, 68, 70, 79, 82–4, 104, 113–16
Guest, Mathew 26, 28
Gutierrez, Gustavo 15

Hammersley, Martyn 31, 42
Hauerwas, Stanley 110
Heitink, Gerben 19
Hermeneutics, congregational 49
Hiltner, Seward 10, 12–13
Historical theology 10–11, 18, 36, 104, 106, 108, 111, 119, 127
Holy Spirit, the 7, 47, 93
Home groups 40, 45, 48, 51, 62–3, 68, 76, 81, 130
Homosexuality 59, 87
Honesty 64, 72–3, 78–9, 81
Hopewell, James 3, 26–9, 125
Hospitality 59

Idiom 27
Individualism 71, 106
Informal interviews (*see* "Data collection")
Integrated Wayfinders 60, 84
Interviews (*see* "Data collection")

Jacobsfield 38, 56–7
Jacobsfield Furniture Project 41, 49, 70, 72, 87, 130
Jamieson, Alan 59–60, 76–7, 83–4, 99, 106, 109, 114, 117, 123
Journey (course) 50–52, 105

Kingdom of God 112, 116, 121

Lartey, Emmanuel 21
Lawton, Matt 6, 8, 37–41, 45–53, 56, 60–5, 67–71, 73–4, 76, 78–81, 83–5, 91, 96–8, 105, 108–13, 120
LeCompte, Margaret 32,
Liminality
  History of 107
Liminal groups/churches 70, 77, 83–5, 99, 106–8, 111, 115, 117, 126
Loder, James Edwin 34, 36

Marginal groups 83–4, 117, 123
Marty, Martin 23
Maturity i, 67, 69–70, 72, 82–84, 87, 91–2, 98–99, 104, 113–17, 126, 132
McCann, Dennis 15–17
McLaren, Brian 5, 50, 108
Metanarrative 115, 119–21
Methodism 61, 108
Miller, Donald 28
Mission 6, 22–5, 64, 101, 106, 108–9, 112, 116, 119–22, 125, 127
Modernism 2–4, 19, 65, 74, 95, 97, 105
Mowat, Harriet 22, 36
Mudge, Lewis 27
Mumford, John 37
Murphy, Nancey 119–20

Narrative 27–8, 30, 36–7, 39, 44–5, 51, 66, 68
Naturalism 101
Norms 34, 77, 97, 99, 101, 109, 117

Ogletree, Thomas 16, 18–19
Openness 72, 78–9, 81
Other, the 77, 117–18, 120–22

Palmer, Parker J. 23
Participant observation 28, 41, 43–5, 67, 71, 91
Pattison, Stephen 8, 14–16, 22, 25
Peirce, Charles 102–3
Poling, James 28
Positivism 101–2
Post-modernism
  Churches 64, 88
  Culture/people 1, 6, 61, 65, 92, 120, 127, 129, 131
  Philosophy 3–4, 73, 83, 88, 97, 105
  Theology 65, 119–20,
Power 29, 51, 67, 71, 80–81, 83, 132
Practical theology
  Adopted definition and model 24–6
  Common characteristics 14–23, 42
  Historical development 8–9
  Purpose 21–3, 91–2, 101, 103, 106, 121, 124
  Reflection 101, 103–4, 111, 114, 116–17, 120–21, 124, 126–7
  Relationship to congregational studies 25–6, 28–31, 125
  Relationship to ethnography 31–4, 101
  Relationship with the social sciences 34–6, 43–4, 101
  Various approaches 8–14, 23–4
Praxis
  Definitions of 15–17, 19, 32–3
  Ecclesial 24–5, 31–2, 42, 49, 109, 122, 124–5
Prayer 9, 22, 29, 39, 46–8, 50, 67, 83, 86, 89, 97, 117, 132
Preissle, Judith 32
Prophecy 112
Protestant Reformation 9, 108, 121

Questioning 71, 78, 81, 120

Rahner, Karl 12
Realness 63–5, 70, 72, 79, 81–2, 91, 109–10, 114

Reconstruction
  Challenges of i, 108, 122–4
  Crisis of 78, 92, 98–9
  Criteria for 59, 100, 104
Reflective Exiles 60, 83
Relevance i, 1, 52, 61, 64, 69–70, 73, 78, 85–7, 92, 98–101, 104, 109, 117, 122, 124, 127
Religious parentage i, 3, 104–9, 122
Ricoeur, Paul 99
Riddell, Mike 2
Rites of passage 107, 114
Robson, Colin 44
Roozen, David 24
Ryle, Gilbert 33

Safe places i, 74, 79, 104, 109–12, 114
Schleiermacher, Friedrich 10–11, 119
Schreiter, Robert 21, 29–30, 33, 106
Schweitzer, Friedrich 15, 34–5, 116
Semi-structured interviews (*see* "Data collection")
Sensitizing concepts 101–2
Sermons (talks) 47–9, 52, 67, 69, 80–81, 95, 97–8, 120
Sexual ethics 76, 104
Situations, Interpretation of 13, 16, 18–25, 32–4, 44, 101, 110, 112, 116–17, 120, 122, 124–5
Small groups (*see* home groups)
Social sciences 14, 19, 21, 23, 25, 28, 31–2, 34–6, 101, 103
Southwest London Vineyard 37–8, 95
Spirituality
  Curiosity and interest in 1, 25, 61, 118
  JV conceptions 64, 68–9, 73, 83, 87–8, 95
  "Messy spirituality" 51, 67, 70, 79, 83, 99, 113, 114, 132
Spradley, James 32
Stokes, Alison 25
Strauss, Anselm 102–3
Stringer, Martin 29, 43
Sunday Services 38, 41, 45–8, 50–52, 56, 62–3, 68–70, 75, 80, 85, 88, 92–3, 97–8, 104–5, 120, 122, 123, 130
Swinton, John 15–17, 22, 36
Systematic theology 10–12, 19, 36, 104, 112, 116, 121

Technology 90, 96, 104, 118–19, 121
Teleology 115–16
Thurneyson, Edward 12, 34
Tillich, Paul 12–13, 19, 35
Tomlinson, Dave 2
Tracy, David 13–17, 21, 33, 35
Transitional Explorers 60, 83–4
Transparency 63, 68, 71, 78, 80–91, 92, 109–10
Triangulation 43–5, 61
Trustees 51, 80
Turner, Victor 77, 107

Van der Ven, Johannes 15, 19
Van Gennep, Arnold 107
Van Maanen, John 32
Vineyard Movement i, 2, 6–8, 37–9, 46–7, 50, 61–4, 67, 69–70, 74, 76, 78, 80, 86, 93–7, 105, 108, 132

Wagner, C. Peter 3
Wheeler, Barbara 26
Wimber, John 7, 37, 63, 93
Woodward, James 8, 14, 22, 25
Worship 3–4, 6–7, 29–30, 38, 40, 44, 46–7, 53, 62–3, 67, 69, 77, 80, 83, 88, 91–8, 104, 120, 122, 126, 132

Yaconelli, Mike 51